DISCARDED

MEMBERS, ORGANIZATION AND PERFORMANCE

For Chungwei, Joshua, and Julian
Ad Majorem Dei Gloriam

Members, Organization and Performance
An empirical analysis of the impact of party membership size

ALEXANDER C. TAN
University of North Texas

Ashgate
Aldershot • Burlington USA • Singapore • Sydney

© Alexander C. Tan 2000

All rights reserved. No part of this publication may be reproduced, stored in a retrieval system or transmitted in any form or by any means, electronic, mechanical, photocopying, recording or otherwise without the prior permission of the publisher.

Published by
Ashgate Publishing Limited
Gower House
Croft Road
Aldershot
Hampshire GU11 3HR
England

Ashgate Publishing Company
131 Main Street
Burlington, VT 05401-5600 USA

Ashgate website: http://www.ashgate.com

British Library Cataloguing in Publication Data
Tan, Alexander C.
  Members, organization and performance : an empirical
  analysis of the impact of party membership size
  1. Party affiliation
  I. Title
  324.2

Library of Congress Control Number: 00-134831

ISBN 0 7546 1418 2

Printed and bound by Athenaeum Press, Ltd.,
Gateshead, Tyne & Wear.

Contents

List of Abbreviations vi
List of Figures vii
List of Tables viii
Acknowledgements x

1 The Study of Party Size 1

2 Extant Theories of the Impact of Party Size 16

3 Empirical Tests of the Cross-sectional Model 28

4 Toward a Dynamic Theory of Party Size 50

5 Empirical Tests and Analysis of the Dynamic Model 61

6 Conclusion 78

Bibliography 85

Appendix I List of Political Parties 98

Appendix II Coding Scheme for Leadership Concentration 100

List of Abbreviations

ARP	Dutch Anti-Revolutionary Party
CDA	Christian Democratic Appeal
CDU	German Christian Democrats
CHU	Christian Historical Union
DNA	Norwegian Labour Party
FDP	German Free Democrats
FPO	Austrian Freedom Party
H	Norwegian Conservative Party
ICPP	International Comparative Political Parties project
KESK	Finnish Agrarian Union
KOK	Finnish Conservative National Coalition
KRF	Norwegian Progress Party
KVP	Dutch Catholic People's Party
NSF	United States National Science Foundation
OLS	Ordinary least squares regression
OVP	Austrian People's Party
SD	Social Democrats
SDP	Finnish Social Democrats
SFP	Finnish People's Party
SKDL	Finnish Communist Party
SP	Norwegian Centre Party
SPD	German Social Democrats
SPO	Austrian Socialist Party
STV	Single transferable vote
V	Norwegian Liberals

List of Figures

Figure 2.1	Cross-sectional Model of the Impact of Party Membership Size	17
Figure 4.1	Inverse of the Cross-sectional Model	51
Figure 4.2	Dynamic Model of Party Membership Size Change	52

List of Tables

Table 1.1	Levels of Party Membership Compared	7
Table 1.2	Levels of Party Membership by Party	8
Table 1.3	Number of New Parties Established After 1965	10
Table 3.1	Organizational Complexity Scores	34
Table 3.2	Centralization of Power Scores	35
Table 3.3	Concentration of Power Scores	36
Table 3.4	Intra-party Democratic Performance Scores	37
Table 3.5	Regression Results of Organizational Complexity	39
Table 3.6	Regression Results of Centralization of Power	41
Table 3.7	Regression Results of Concentration of Power	42
Table 3.8	Regression Results of Intra-party Participation	45
Table 4.1	Number of Party Staff	55
Table 5.1	Coding Scheme for Intra-party Democratic Performance	65
Table 5.2	Summary Statistics	66
Table 5.3	Determinants of Organization Complexity	68

| Table 5.4 | Determinants of Centralization of Power | 70 |
| Table 5.5 | Determinants of Intra-party Democratic Performance | 72 |

Acknowledgements

This work benefitted tremendously from Bob Harmel's insightful comments and critiques of my dissertation which this book is largely based upon. He, along with Ken Janda, generously shared their Party Change project data for the empirical analysis used in this book. This book has also benefitted from the generosity of Misha Taylor and Rob Bohrer in sharing their precious time in reading earlier versions of this manuscript to make it more cogent and readable.

In the past few years, I have presented parts of this work in several political science conferences here in the United States. Parts of Chapter 3 were presented at the Western Political Science Association annual meeting in Portland, Oregon and has benefitted from the comments and suggestions of William Eubank. A portion of Chapter 5 was presented at the Southern Political Science Association annual meeting in Atlanta, Georgia. This particular chapter has benefitted tremendously from Dan Ward's comments and suggestions. Dan went beyond the call of duty of a panel discussant to correspond with me on how I can improve and strengthen the analysis and arguments I have made.

I have also sent out various versions and parts of the manuscript to colleagues who have generously spared their time to provide valuable comments and suggestions. I thank Lars Svasand and Susan Scarrow whose insightful comments and breadth of knowledge of the literature has always been tremendously helpful. Bill Bernhard who as a friend has been a good source of encouragement and has provided suggestions that helped in the arguments made in Chapter 5.

Many scholars have read various parts and versions of this project and have directly offered comments, suggestions, and encouragement. In particular, I thank Russ Dalton, John D. Robertson, Thomas Poguntke, Harland Prechel, and Jan Leighley. Thanks are also due to Ashgate's external reviewer for his comments on the initial book proposal.

At the University of North Texas, I thank my colleague Steve Poe who as my 'unofficial' senior faculty mentor has been a constant source of support and encouragement. I acknowledge the timely assistance of my colleague, Karl Ho and my students, Dawn Miller, Elaine Takacs and Tsung-chi Yu. And at Ashgate, thanks are due to Kirstin Howgate and

Anne Keirby for their assistance in the production of this book.

Families are always an important element of one's work and mine is no exception. I would like to thank my everdearest wife, Chungwei, for her unconditional love, prayers, and encouragement. Her encouraging words at critical junctures of the project and assistance in proofreading the whole manuscript helped push it to its completion. My sons, Joshua and Julian, are still too young to read this work but they think it is 'cool' that their dad is writing a book. I thank them for understanding that dad cannot play with them all the time because he has to write. I hope, though, that they may gain some satisfaction in reading the work that took away some of my time with them. To them I dedicate this work.

Corinth, Texas
A. C. Tan

1 The Study of Party Size

The Research Question

What is the impact of declining party size on a political party's democratic and electoral performance? This is the primary question that motivates this study. This book will provide empirical evidence to answer the above question.

In 1911, Michels asserted that the dramatic expansion of party membership within the German Social Democratic Party had influenced the development of a complex and hierarchical organization and a subsequent decline in intra-party democracy. Other scholars have examined the effect of growing party size on electoral performance. With the decline in party membership in many Western European democracies (Katz 1987; Widfeldt 1992), Michels' model could be taken to imply that the relationships observed during decline should be simply the opposites of those during growth and expansion, i.e., an increase in intra-party democracy as size and organizational complexity declines. Yet, in a dynamic setting, there is no a priori reason for us to expect that the impacts of decline in party size are simply the reverse of those of expanding party size.

Numerous studies have analyzed the decline of party membership, while none have studied the impact of this decline on party organizations themselves. More particularly, the primary concern of this study is the impact of decline in party size on a political party's democratic and electoral performance. A secondary concern of this study is to examine the impact of declining party size on a party's organizational form, e.g., complexity and centralization.

It is in that context that this book examines the relationship of party size with organizational attributes found in a political party. More specifically, this study addresses the questions: Is party size critical in determining organizational complexity? Do changes in party size and organizational complexity impact upon the electoral and democratic performance of a political party? What are the impacts of changes in the organizational attributes on the distribution of power within the party? In answering these questions (particularly the last two) we are attempting to connect the study of party size to the broader and more fundamental issue of party transformation and adaptation that is observed in Western political parties and its consequent impact on party organization and performance.

The Study of Party Size and Party Organization

Robert Michels' classic work on the German Social Democratic Party more' than eighty years ago focused on the development of the political party as an organization. In this seminal work Michels asserted that the development of organization and the subsequent establishment of its leadership tends to alter, if not stifle, the internal cohesion and participatory aspects of a political party. This process actually involves a two-stage approach, the first of which focuses on the factors that lead to the development of the organization, which is then followed by a subsequent analysis of the impact of organization on the quality of internal participation. Despite Michel's insightful work, however, studies of political parties as organizations have taken a back seat to the more popular studies of voting behavior and coalition theory that were influenced by rational choice and the behavioral revolution in political science.

Simultaneously, students of organization in other fields of social science (particularly sociology) have increasingly focused their research agenda in an attempt to comprehend the development of complex social organizations. Early effort was focused on examining and discovering the critical forces that influence the development of organizational structure. Among these many studies, attention has often been drawn to the importance of organizational size for the development of organizational structure (Blau 1970; Blau and Schoenherr 1971; Pugh, Hickson, Hinnings and Turner 1968; Child and Mansfield 1972; Mileti, Gillespie, and Haas 1977; Hall, Haas, and Johnson 1967).[1] Ironically, these works, while not directly influenced by Michels, are akin to Michels' first stage of discovering the critical forces that influence the development of organizational structure.

Interestingly, most works along these lines have neglected the study of political parties as an organization (see Janda 1983, 321-322). Panebianco charges that "most contemporary analyses resist studying parties for what they obviously are: organizations" (1988, 3). Albinsson (1986; 184) laments that not only are organization theorists at fault for neglecting the study of political parties, but students of political parties themselves have failed to see the utility of organization theory for their own studies (also see Janda 1983, 321-325).

Gibson et al. (1983, 196) lament that advancement of a theory of party organizations has been impeded by a lack of emphasis on comparative research. While research on the U.S. parties has been comparative at the state level, little has been done at the cross-national level. Except for the cross-national study by Harmel and Janda (1982) in their book *Parties and their Environments* it is safe to say that there have been very few systematic cross-national studies of party organizations (see also Janda 1979; Janda and Janda 1985). In fact the current published literature that resulted directly from the Katz and Mair (1994) cross-national project on party organization has failed thus far to rigorously compare across countries on the scale that has been done by Harmel and Janda's earlier work.[2]

In this study I will focus on the impact of party size on party organizations by using a cross-national sample of Western industrial democracies. Before doing so, however, I will make the case for the study of my main independent variable - party size. In this discussion I will highlight some problems - both conceptual and empirical - that have limited studies of party size in the past.

Scholars frequently cite decreasing party membership and partisanship as evidence that political parties are declining (Dalton, Flanagan, and Beck 1984; Sainsbury 1985; Katz 1987; Messina 1995). Despite the concern about party decline though, research has only focused on the declining linkage between political parties and civil society (Katz and Mair 1995 and others). Incredibly, no questions have been raised regarding the impact of this decline in party size on how political parties organize.

Why Party Size?

The impact of organizational size on other organizational attributes is well established within the studies of complex organizations (Blau 1970; Blau and Schoenherr 1971; Tsouderos 1955; Ford 1980a, 1980b; Hall, Haas, and Johnson 1967). Yet, within the study of political parties, empirical study of party size and particularly its impact on organization has not generated the same obvious interest.[3] Why? This dearth of attention can be attributed to two main factors, one conceptual and the other empirical.

Conceptually, the idea of party size is rather nebulous. Debate swirls around the definition of party size. What is party size? How do we measure it? To some scholars size simply denotes the number of members a party claims to have, while for others party size would include the number of supporters and voters within the electorate (see Muller-Rommel and Pridham 1991).[4] A related problem is whether or not party size also includes the members of ancillary organizations and corporate members as well as direct members (Smith 1991; Widfeldt 1992).

One convenient method of understanding party size is to examine political parties in three different but related dimensions. Katz and Mair (1995) suggest that we need to move away from the exclusive conception of party as a unitary actor and the concern with the relationship between parties and society in general. They suggest that party organizations should be viewed with three faces which include the party in public office, the party on the ground, and the party in central office. They further argue, however, that in the case of most political parties organized as mass parties, the party in central office and the party on the ground can be combined. Indeed, understanding of these distinctions should help students of political parties in adopting a particular definition (and consequently the operationalization) of party size.

It is essential to take note, though, that the debate regarding party size helps in clarifying the concept of political party size. This study is fundamentally interested in the internal facets and features of political parties and the consequent impact of party size on other organizational attributes. In the jargon that Katz and Mair have suggested then, this study is primarily interested in the membership party and the party in central office. In this regard, Widfeldt suggests that "direct membership is the most straightforward (or least roundabout) way of describing the membership size of a party" (1992, 9).

Blondel, in arguing about the primacy of direct individual membership in political parties, stated that

> individual membership has long been thought to be the basis and main characteristic of modern political parties...membership is held to be the result of the voluntary and indeed deliberate action of individuals wishing to show that they approve of a party ideology and programme (1978, 145).

Relatedly, the empirical impediments of studies in party size stem largely from the problems associated with the conceptual vagueness of the phenomenon. The vagueness of the concept becomes evident as one attempts to measure party size. Yet, if one subscribes to Katz and Mair's prescription about the three "faces" of parties then part of this empirical problem can be adequately resolved by equating party size with the size of party membership. The other half of the problem mainly deals with measurement and the quality of the data.

In spite of these problems, there is arguably a need to study party size and its impact on organizations. Firstly, the need to study party size can be attributed to the prominence of size as an explanatory factor in the studies of complex organizations. Students of organizations, dating as far back as Michels, have suggested that size can explain how complex organizations organize. Indeed to understand party organizations, all organizational attributes need to be examined.

Panebianco observes that while "almost no empirical research has been done on the influence of size on parties, party literature is full of observations about it" (1988, 186). He argues, though, that many of these observations have missed the mark. "Size in and of itself does not seem responsible for significant variations in political style, participation, complexity or bureaucratization" (Panebianco 1988, 190). He further explains that

> Even if growth were the main cause of internal complexity, we still could not substantiate the close connection between them asserted by Michels and Blau. We would still have to demonstrate that (1) when size decreases, complexity and/or the level of bureaucratization diminish at the same time; (2) that a big organization is always more complex than a small one (1988, 189).

Despite these sweeping claims, Panebianco offers only anectodal evidence. This study will address these issues in a systematic manner by providing empirical tests of whether size does indeed affect other organizational attributes and, second, provide a dynamic analysis using a cross-national sample of political parties from Western industrial nations.

Secondly, beyond the examination of the empirical relationships between organizational size and other organizational attributes, little has been done (particularly in studies of political parties) to place this issue in the broader context of party transformation, decline or adaptation. The need to study party size and its consequent impact on how parties organize lies in the heart of our understanding of political parties as linkage mechanism between civil society and the state (Widfeldt 1999). As Western democracies witness tremendous changes, their citizens have been less likely to take their identities from parties, political parties are demanded to be able to "engage in permanent innovation and experiment" (Jacques 1995, 104).[5] This continual innovation and transformation required of political parties will undoubtedly affect the organizational structure and distribution of power.[6] More importantly, these same changes may even transform the traditional role and functions of political parties in democratic political systems. Based on the empirical findings of this study, I will reflect on the transformation in the role and functions of political parties in an era which many political observers call the "end of politics."

The Problem of Shrinking Party Size

Are parties really in decline? When talking about the decline of parties, one conjures up images of the irrelevance of political parties to a democratic political system. Another image that one may associate with the party decline thesis is the declining levels of party identification in the electorate. The American party literature (primarily in the political behavior literature) is replete with this second image where discussions of declining partisanship of the electorate are seen as signs of declining significance of political parties. Particularly telling is the observation that Americans have been shunning identification with the major parties but have been rather active in alternative forms of political participation other than voting (Dalton 1996).[7]

Scholars have prophesied the decline of political parties in Western democracies (Epstein 1967). Most often, the key evidence cited by proponents of the party decline thesis is the political parties' dwindling "ability to engage people in long-term mobilization" (Widfeldt 1992, 2). Parties are assumed to "like as large a membership as possible" (Widfeldt 1992, 2) but are increasingly unable to entice the populace to join the cause (Scarrow 1996). In fact, in other Western industrial democracies, there has been a relative decline in the levels of party membership.

As can be seen from Table 1.1, there has been a general decline or stagnancy (except for Belgium and Germany) in the overall level of party membership (i.e., cumulated across a system's parties) in selected West European industrial democracies. The decline is modest in some countries, e.g., Sweden, but in general many West European party systems have experienced substantial decline in the ratio of party members vis-a-vis the total electorate.

Table 1.1   Levels of Party Membership Compared
(selected Western industrial democracies)

	1960-69 % of electorate	1980-89 % of electorate
Austria	26.2	21.8
Belgium	8.0	9.0
Denmark	21.1	6.5
Finland	19.0	15.0
France	2.0	3.0
Germany	2.7	4.2
Ireland	5.0	5.0
Italy	13.0	10.0
Netherlands	9.4	2.9
Norway	15.0	15.0
Sweden	22.0	21.2
Switzerland	25.0	10.0
UK	9.4	3.3

Source: Mair 1994; Katz and Mair 1992; Hermet, Hottinger, and Seiler 1998.

Even with these indicative data, however, the measurement of partisanship at the system level may mask the true extent of shrinking membership at the organization level (see Selle and Svasand 1991 for the Norwegian case). At the system level the transformation in the level of party membership may not be as impressive, yet the decline in party membership can be better observed in the fluctuations in membership in each of the parties within a system. The data in Table 1.2 substantiate my argument. Except for the German parties, most party systems in the sample have parties that have seen decline in the levels of party membership. The two British parties and the Danish parties are cases in point. The Labour Party laid claim to more than 680,000 members in the 1970 but this figure

Table 1.2 Levels of Party Membership by Party ('000)

Country	Party	1970	1989
Austria	SPO	719	597
	OVP	561	497
	FPO	27	39
Denmark	SD	177	98
	Venstre	136	79
	Conservative	129	40
	Social Liberal	25	9
Finland	SKDL	51	33
	SDP	60	85
	KESK	288	286
	SFP	49	45
	KOK	81	70
Germany	CDU	329	662
	FDP	56	65
	SPD	820	921
Netherlands	Labour	107[a]	96
	ARP/CHU/KVP (CDA)	207	125
	Liberal	38	64
Norway	DNA	106[b]	96
	H	146[b]	146
	KRF	67[b]	56
	SP	70	44
	V	13	11
Sweden	SD	1028[c]	978
	Center	116	112
	People's	76	43
	Moderate	61	77
U.K.	Conservative	1500[d]	750
	Labour	680	293

Source: Katz and Mair 1992.
[a] 1969 figure; [b] 1979 figure; [c] 1976 figure; [d] 1974 figure.

dropped to less than 300,000 in 1989. Although membership figures for the Conservative Party are not complete, the available data show that membership has declined to less than half of that in the 1960s. In fact, in 1974 the British Conservative Party claims a membership of 1.5 million but in 1989 can only claim half of this figure. In the case of the Danish parties, all parties experienced decline party membership levels.

Yet, despite these shrinking membership statistics students of political parties continue to argue that political parties remain relevant to the political system, albeit undergoing certain transformations with regard to their relation to civil society. Dalton (1996), in his study of citizen participation in four Western democracies, observes that political parties remain the primary organizational actors in the political system. Parties, he argues, are

> the primary institutions of representative democracy, especially in Europe. Parties define the structure of electoral competition. Candidates in most European nations are selected by the parties and elected as party representatives, not as individuals. Open primaries and independent legislators are virtually unknown outside the United States. A large proportion of Europeans (including the Germans) vote directly for party lists and not for individual candidates. Once in government, parties exercise control over the policymaking process. This control is often absolute, as in the parliamentary systems of Europe...American parties are less united and less decisive, but even here parties are the prime factors structuring the legislative process...Parties also perform an education function by informing the public. More generally, E.E. Schattschneider once concluded that democracy without parties is unthinkable (1996, 143-144).

These functions (enumerated by Dalton) continue to be performed by political parties. In spite of criticism of political parties' organizational conservatism and inability to change with the times, Jacques (like E.E. Schattschneider) acknowledged that "it is difficult to imagine a political system without parties" (1995, 104). Political parties remain the primary access vehicles for participating in elections, controlling government and public policy. In fact, Western industrial democracies have witnessed the birth of several new parties, thereby countering arguments that political parties are declining in relevance.

Table 1.3 presents the number of new political parties that have been established in a sample of Western industrial democracies in or after

1965. Observing the data presented in Table 1-3, the Western democracies included in the sample have witnessed the creation of new political parties in contrary to the "frozen party system" thesis formulated by Lipset and Rokkan (1967). In Germany for example, by the end of 1984 24 new political parties had been established. The German figure is high even when compared to the other countries. Nonetheless, most countries have seen at least three new political parties established since 1965.

Table 1.3   Number of New Parties Established After 1965
(for selected Western industrial democracies)

Country	Number of parties
Australia	3
Austria	4
Canada	5
Denmark	7
Germany	24
Netherlands	11
New Zealand	6
Sweden	3
UK	6

Source: Alan J. Day and Henry W. Degenhart (eds.). 1984. *Political Parties of the World*.
Note: The number of new parties listed here are just the surviving parties as of the book's publication deadline.

It is in the context of the evidence of new parties being established in Western democracies that Selle and Svasand assert that

> The emergence of new parties can clearly be seen as indicating that the political party as such is not an obsolete strategy for interest articulation...Obviously, some of the new parties may not necessarily be formed for the purpose of winning elections. The interesting fact, nevertheless, is that the idea of having parties is not in decline, although there may be dissatisfaction with established parties or with the political system (1991, 470).

Indeed, the continuing creation of new parties despite the shrinking of party membership does not seem to support the party decline thesis very well (Reiter 1989). Instead of "party decline" it may well be thought of as party transformation or adaptation. Also citing shrinking party membership but offering a contrasting thesis, Katz and Mair (1995) in their numerous studies of party change argue that political parties are not in decline but instead are undergoing a fundamental transformation. The perspective they take is that political parties are increasingly becoming associated with the state such that parties survive because of the state and vice versa. One consequence of this change is that political parties may *not want* so many members in the first place such that they have actually decided to downsize. Party elites may determine that large membership does not necessarily bring benefits to the party that increasing party professionalization could not also achieve. Even if members may be valuable to the organization, they are not necessarily costless. Besides the material costs of recruiting and other organizational overhead, members may impose costs on the party elites by limiting their freedom of maneuver (Katz 1990, 153). Consequently, Katz explains that "the balance of costs and benefits of party membership is shifting in Europe, both for political party elites and for ordinary citizens, and that the effect of that shift is to make membership less attractive for both" (1990, 158). Rather than asserting that decreasing party membership signals the decline of political parties, it is suggested that the trend is partly an indication "of a more general evolution [towards] 'new politics'" (Katz 1990, 158; see Scarrow 1994 for an alternative perspective).

In a later work, Katz and Mair (1995) contend that we are witnessing an evolution in political party models in the party systems of Western industrial democracies. Moreover, it is suggested that Duverger's (1963) mass party model and Kirchheimer's (1966) catch-all party model may be relics of the past. Instead since political parties have increasingly found themselves associated with the state, cartel party may become the model of the future (Katz and Mair 1995). In Katz and Mair's conception, cartel parties are characterized by less members (compared to the mass or catch-all party). Furthermore this type of political party is more technology-intensive in disseminating its electoral positions, principles or ideology. Katz and Mair and many others have argued that the roles of members within a political party have been increasingly replaced by the reliance on experts and consultants and the use of communications and electronic technology employed by the political parties; i.e, political parties are becoming more professionalized. Consequently, this group of scholars would argue that parties do not necessarily want to carry the burden of too many members; hence the decline in political party membership.[8]

Whether one subscribes to Katz and Mair's cartel party model or not,[9] one must recognize the serious issues and implications raised by the fact that parties from a historical context are declining in size both in absolute terms and in a relative sense vis-a-vis the size of the electorate. One implication of these changes is that political parties are shedding their traditional image as aggregators and articulators of varied interests. In the cartel party model, political parties are increasingly becoming more professionalized at the expense of membership. This has obvious implications for organizational structure which have not been examined cross-nationally.

The question remains, therefore, whether the evolution of political parties and its resulting effects on party membership size has impacted upon the way political parties organize themselves. Due to the growth orientation of the extant literature, many scholars have ignored the fact that organizations may undergo evolutionary phases of birth, growth, stability, *and decline* (Ford 1980a, 589). While the study of party models is important in itself, many party scholars have not studied the impact of party *decline* on the organization and on its democratic and electoral performance.

Yet, there have been numerous speculations about the probable impact of party decline on organization. Selle and Svasand (1991, 474), in a study of Norwegian parties, observe that

> the increasing volatility, or lack of deeply-felt loyalty, also gives the party leadership greater political maneuverability, both in terms of reorganization (organizational change) and reorientation (political and ideological change), because the direct control and possible sanctions of members are not very strong. The lower cost of exit probably also changes the relationship between exit and voice in favor of increasing exit at the expense of voice.

It is exactly changes in the relationship between membership and party leadership that are bound to be reflected in the organizational changes taking place within political parties. Furthermore, these changes may impact upon the distribution of power within the political parties, between the different levels of party organization but also the concentration of power in the hands of central party leaders.

"The issue of party decline is, therefore, not only a matter of establishing time-series data for appropriate indicators but also of relating such indicators to organizational changes in the parties and to contextual factors that may modify their impact" (Selle and Svasand 1991, 474). In spite of the keen and insightful observations of Selle and Svasand, much remains to be done in the study of the impact of party decline on party organizations, in both a dynamic and cross-national approach. With the availability of several new data collection projects, this is exactly what this study sets out to achieve.

In summary, although many scholars have examined various aspects of party size and organizational structure, no authors have assembled the whole puzzle to form a complete picture of the interrelationships of these various variables and how they impact parties' democratic and electoral performance. In the following chapter, the cross-sectional model will be presented in its entirety as identified from the current literature.

The Structure of the Book

In Chapter Two I will first formulate the cross-sectional model identified from the extant literature in political science and studies of complex organization that deal with various aspects of organization size, other organizational attributes, and organizational performance. I will then present and test the various theories and hypotheses that have been identified in a survey of the extant literature. The purpose of this initial exercise is twofold: firstly, to present a holistic picture of the various relationships of organizational attributes and the forces affecting them; and secondly, to provide empirical tests of these relationships in political parties.

In Chapter Three, the cross-sectional model and the hypotheses identified will be systematically tested using Janda's International Comparative Political Parties (ICPP) data which cover the period 1950-1962 and Katz and Mair's Party Organizations data set covering the period 1960-1990. The ICPP dataset includes indicators such as organizational complexity, centralization of power, membership involvement, etc. - attributes which are incorporated in the cross-sectional model. While the ICPP data set covers both developed and developing countries of that time period, this study will only concentrate on Western industrial democracies included in the ICPP project and the Party Organizations project.[10]

The empirical test and theoretical clarification of the cross-sectional model in Chapter Three lead to the more fundamental objective of this study which is to examine some conceptual and theoretical challenges to the relationships presented in the cross-sectional model which is the main focus of Chapter Four. Chapter Five presents the empirical test of the hypotheses set forth in Chapter Four. The challenge to the existing cross-sectional model asks whether the relationships as identified in the extant literature, and as presented in the cross-sectional model, hold in the broader context of changes in the level of party membership. In other words, do the relationships found earlier when studying growing parties remain true in the dynamic environment observed today in many Western political parties? More particularly, in the face of declining membership and downsizing of political parties, we need to examine what these changes signify to a political party's organizational complexity and, ultimately, to its performance.

On the basis of these findings, we will be equipped with an understanding of the impacts of the changes in the various factors on political party structures. In the concluding chapter, I discuss their implications of these empirical findings on the transformation of the role of political parties as we know it.

Notes

1. In longitudinal studies of organizational size, several scholars have argued that organizational size can lead to inertia. In other words, large organizations are less likely to change (see Ford 1980a). Since this literature deals with dynamics rather than statics, I will briefly mention them in the discussion leading to the dynamic model of party size. In this introductory section, I simply lay out past studies that have dealt with size in a "static" sense.

2. For examples of more recent cross-national work on change in party organization, see Harmel, Heo, Tan and Janda 1995; Janda, Harmel, Edens and Goff 1995.

3. There are several recent works that have studied some aspects of party membership size (see Scarrow 1996 and Widfeldt 1999) but these works have not specifically looked at the impact of party membership size on the party organization.

4. While numerous party scholars argue that political parties are unique forms of organizations, the conceptual and empirical debates about organization size is not unique to political parties. In the study of complex organizations, specifically business organizations and government agencies, similar debates have occurred (Blau 1970; Pugh, Hickson, Hinnings

and Turner 1968).

5. Jacques (1995) attributes the crisis of politics in Western societies to the decline of the state, and the decline in the importance of the traditional left-right polarity. The decline of the left-right polarity has been caused by the decline of the working class population and the decline in the importance of ideology.

6. See Prechel 1991 and references in the article for discussions on organizational transformation in studies of complex organizations in sociology.

7. Dalton (1996) notes that as a result of the growing political sophistication of citizens communal activity (e.g. citizen contacting) in France, Germany, the U.K. and the U.S. have been observed to be increasing. These types of activities are said to be more citizen initiated, less structured as in party activities and more policy oriented.

8. For a counter-argument of why parties continue to recruit members see Scarrow (1994, 1996).

9. For a counter-argument on the cartel party thesis, see Ruud Koole (1996).

10. Data availability is an important issue in this study. The Party Organizations data set only covers a limited number of Western industrial democracies. For the empirical test, the countries that are in common in both the ICPP data set and the Party Organizations data set were chosen.

2 Extant Theories of the Impact of Party Size

As discussed in the preceding chapter, in order for us to fully comprehend how political parties organize we would need to understand the effect of party size on party organization and intra-party democratic performance. In this chapter I first set out to formulate the relevant hypotheses as suggested in the extant literature and then, in order to control for the effects of the environment, I briefly discuss the impact of the relevant environmental factors on party organization.

Party-level Factors and Organizational Attributes

Party Size and Structure

Michels (1962) discussed extensively the impact of party size on the quality of participation of members within a political party. More specifically, he argued that the development of organization as a result of the growth in size may impede democratic participation or the meaningful involvement of the party's members. What causes the organization to develop a complex and hierarchical structure in the first place? What are the factors that lead to the development of complex organization?[1]

From Michels' study of the German Social Democratic Party (SPD) we can logically infer that the size of the organization definitely has an impact on the organization. In his study of the SPD, Michels argued that the need for organization arises because it is impossible to carry out the party tasks without an organized system of representation. Michels suggested that "where the labor party sometimes numbers its adherents by tens of thousands, it is impossible to carry on the affairs of this gigantic body without a system of representation" (1962, 65). In a similar vein, Blondel suggests that as parties develop and grow they come to "need a considerable number of sub-leaders, or cadres which...organize and supervise large numbers of small cells (or sections) which together constitute the party" (1978, 148).

Figure 2.1 Cross-sectional Model of the Impact of Party Membership Size

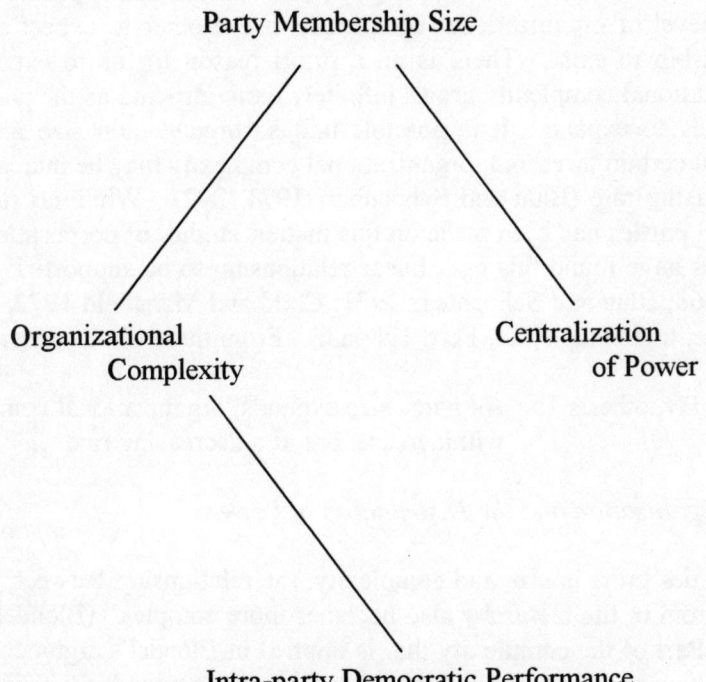

It is interesting to note that both Michels and Blondel seem to argue that the development of organization implies that organizational affairs will be managed more efficiently. In fact, Michels asserts that "it is obvious that such a gigantic number of persons belonging to a unitary organization cannot do any practical work upon a system of direct discussion" (1962, 65), thereby implying that some form of hierarchical and complex structure may be developed to make organizational activity more effective.[2]

Nonetheless, it is one thing to posit that size has a positive effect on the level of organizational complexity and another to expect a linear relationship to exist. There is no a priori reason for us to expect that organizational complexity grows infinitely more intricate as the party size continues to expand. It is possible that as organization size increases beyond a certain threshold, organizational complexity may be increasing at a decreasing rate (Blau and Schoenherr 1971, 302). While no study on political parties has been made on this matter, studies of corporations and agencies have found this curvilinear relationship to be supported[3] (Pugh et al 1968; Blau and Schoenherr 1971; Child and Mansfield 1972; Mileti, Gillespie, and Haas 1977; Ford 1980a,b). From these discussions, I posit

Hypothesis 1: As party size expands, organizational complexity will increase, but at a decreasing rate.

Size, Organization and the Distribution of Power

"As parties grow in size and complexity, the relationship between the top and bottom of the hierarchy also becomes more complex" (Blondel 1978, 148). Part of the complexity that is implied in Blondel's argument is the issue of how power is distributed within the party, particularly between the national organ and the local organs. This is what is referred to in this study as the centralization of power.

Providing a more detailed picture of the transformation in the distribution of power, Michels (1962) argued that the development of the organization leads to the inevitable ascent of technical specialization. With technical specialization, the rise of expert leaders induces a fundamental transformation in the distribution of power within the political party (Michels 1962). As a result, members of a democratic organization experience power being concentrated in the hands of the leaders. It is argued that "the increase in the power of the leaders is directly proportional with the extension of the organization" (Michels 1962, 71). Consequently, as the party increases in size the control exerted by the members increasingly becomes fictitious (Michels 1962, 71). "The price of increased bureaucracy is the concentration of power at the top and the lessening of influence by rank and file members" (Lipset 1962, 16). This implies therefore that as the bureaucracy develops, power increasingly becomes centralized at the top of the hierarchy.

In a later work that primarily examines social action and power and its implications to organization, Weber argues that "power actually rests in the hands of those who, within the organization, handle the work continuously" (Weber 1946, 103). If bureaucratization of the organization simply implies a regularization of procedures and norms, then it follows that bureaucrats are the people directly responsible for the day-to-day operations of the organization. In this regard, it is logical to argue that Weber's contention implies that the rise of bureaucracy within organizations, as well as in political parties, would lead to a centralization and concentration of power.

In a different context and meaning of the term centralization of power, Blondel explains that as the party organization becomes more complex, it contributes more to the decentralized character of the party as many functions are parceled out to "sub-leaders." Then seemingly contradicting his own arguments he suggests that "real decision-making takes place not at these congresses, but in the smaller councils or executives elected at congresses" (Blondel 1978, 149). He further argues that "real difference between party structures is not therefore determined by whether congresses or executives run political parties, but by whether decision-making is centralized at the national level or decentralized so that local and regional bodies are powerful" (Blondel 1978, 149).

For us to be able to compare and give more conceptual clarity to the issue of distribution of power one needs to be able to distinguish between administrative and strategic decisions.[4] Duverger succinctly suggests that "centralization and decentralization define the way in which power is distributed amongst the different levels of leadership" (1963, 52). Despite this clarification, the fundamental confusion of these terms lies in the concept of "power" itself. In this case it is essential that we distinguish between simple administrative decisions and political/strategic decisions. In this study, I will focus on an aspect of "power" that has to do with the making of political and strategic decisions rather than with the implementation of those decisions, which will be "administration" (Harmel 1989, 166).

In light of the discussion above, Panebianco further suggests that "political or strategic decisions (decisions regarding the governing of the organization) are always centralized in bureaucratic organizations" (1988, 200). Michels' and Panebianco's arguments imply, therefore, the existence of two dimensions of power - vertical and horizontal. The vertical relationship involves the power relationship among the layers of organization, while the horizontal relationship involves the number of people making the effective decisions for the national level of the party (see Harmel and Janda 1982, 72; Harmel 1989, 166). It follows from the above that

Hypothesis 2a: The greater the organizational complexity, the greater the centralization of power at the national level.

Hypothesis 2b: The more complex the organization, the more concentrated the power.[5]

Organization and Democratic Performance

For Michels the advance of organization and consequent decline of democracy seems to be an inevitable process even for an organization formed with democratic aspirations. "Every democratic organization rests, by its very nature, upon a division of labor. But wherever division of labor prevails, there is necessarily specialization, and the specialists become indispensable" (Michels 1962, 124). However, "with the advance of organization, democracy tends to decline" (Michels 1962, 70). As was pointed out earlier, specialization and the differentiation of functions lead to increasing bureaucratization of the party. The increasing bureaucratization within the political party results in the decreasing level of internal democracy within the organization (Michels 1962, 70).

Olson (1965) also provides a similar perspective on the effect of group size and level of participation by group members. Olson (1965, 16-36) argues that increasing size of group membership tends to have a negative effect on the level of participation of members, that is, as the size of the group becomes larger members tend to participate less. In other words, large membership in a group does not enhance meaningful participation and encourages free-riding behavior. However, Olson failed to consider the possibility that expansions in membership size may lead to the development of organizational structure and as a result avenues for participation at the varying levels of organizational structure are enhanced. That is, by "dividing up" the organization into several levels and numerous smaller units, the level of participation increases because the number of members in the subgroups decreases. As Blondel argues, contrary to Michels' and Olson's perspectives, that "the development of political parties automatically sows the seeds of some internal responsiveness and internal democracy" (Blondel 1978, 141). Indeed in an empirical analysis using path analytic techniques, Tan (1998, 196) showed that while large party membership size tends to directly dampen the intra-party democratic performance, through its effects on organizational complexity party membership size can indirectly stimulates greater intra-party participation.

Despite these seemingly contradictory assertions in the literature, Harmel (1989) found that the complexity of party organization tends to diminish the level of participation within political parties. We can still posit that,

>   Hypothesis 3:   The greater the organizational complexity, the lower the level of participation.

The preceding sections of this chapter have set forth the relevant testable hypotheses relating to the impact of size and structure on other organizational attributes and performance. In the discussion so far I have only considered the impact of *party level* variables. Indeed in Michels' original conceptualization he only accounts for the impact of party-level factors on the organization itself. Likewise, Tan's (1997; 1998) empirical studies of the impact of party membership, thus far, have not accounted for the impact of environmental factors on party organization. Yet, since political parties as social organizations is endogenous of its operating environment, a complete examination of party organizations necessarily should control for important environmental factors. In the following section, I will discuss the relevance of environmental factors and their impact on how political parties organize. These system level factors will serve as control variables in the empirical tests of the hypotheses presented in the preceding sections.

System Level Determinants of Party Organization

A complete theory of party organizations should account and control for the impact of the environment since the environment obviously affects the shape and behavior of the organization. This is particularly true for political parties where the interactive effects between the organization and the environment are most obvious.

In their extensive research on formal organizations, Blau and Schoenherr exclaimed that

> organizations do not exist in a vacuum but in the context of a social environment...The social context in which organizations are embedded undoubtedly affects their characteristics and their operations. Research on organizations is often criticized for treating them as if they exist in a glass cage and for ignoring the influences of the external situation (1971, 140).

Clarifying further the effects of the systemic factors on the organization, they assert that "the external environment has substantial effects...notably on various aspects of structural differentiation and managerial practices, such as decentralization" (Blau and Schoenherr 1971, 167).

Indeed, to simply study political parties without regard for the greater environment in which they operate is to neglect the possible impact of these systemic factors on party organizations (Harmel 1989; Tan 1995). This neglect may render severe limitations on the validity and generalizability of any empirical findings relating party-level variables to various organizational attributes. On the other hand, to naively appraise "the environment" as a monolithic entirety does not lead us closer to understanding what factors in the environment are relevant determinants of organizations in general and party organizations in particular.

Lawrence and Lorsch (1967) suggest that organizations adapt to a diverse environment by developing a more differentiated internal structure. Many scholars have also suggested that the complexity of organizations will tend to reflect the complexity in their own environments (Blondel 1978; Hall 1977; Katz and Kolodny 1994; Key 1964).

Early studies of party organizations have not really presented rigorous empirical tests but have provided anecdotal evidence to support hypotheses about the impact of systemic-level variables on political parties. As an exception, Harmel and Janda (1982) in *Parties and their Environments* examined the external factors that affect organizational arrangements. An interesting observation one gathers from this extensive cross-national study is that while the environment exerts influence on organizational arrangements, some environmental factors affect party organizations more than others. Harmel and Janda (1982) have identified specific system level factors that influence organizational complexity, centralization of power and performance. In the following discussion, I identify the relevant system level variables and how they affect these specific organizational attributes.

Federalism

In 1964, V.O. Key observed that "party organization is built around the geographic divisions of the country for electoral purposes" (1964, 316) suggesting that party organizations are affected by arrangements of the political system they are operating in. But more than the impact of simple geographic division of a country, as in state or province, some scholars have argued that the type of governmental system has an impact on the ways political parties organize. Epstein suggested that "party organization tends to parallel governmental organization, particularly the governmental organization prevailing when parties originally developed" (1967, 32). More particularly, whether a country is governed as a unitary state or federal state affects the distribution of power between the national and the local organs of political parties.

In claiming that the American party organizations are but an "empty vessel", Katz and Kolodny contend that "the federal nature of American government is also reflected in the organization of the parties" (1994, 29). They further argued that "the most fundamental point about federalism as a factor conditioning the character of American parties is simply that the states are extremely important, both as loci for political careers and as independent decision-makers" (Katz and Kolodny 1994, 27). Due to these factors then American political parties are not only very decentralized but in actuality the national parties are simply "empty vessels."

In earlier work, Blondel (1978) argued a very similar point in his discussion of the impact of governmental arrangement on party distribution of power. In describing the impact of federalism on party decentralization, Blondel asserts that because "federal structure leads to the creation of government-type units in each State or province" parties will organize at the state or provincial level in order to compete for power in these governments. From this observation he then concludes that "federal countries are also those in which the parties' state or provincial organs are strongest" (Blondel 1978, 151), implying that in federal countries political parties are less centralized.

Electoral System

Electoral systems matter. These rules are said to shape not only party organizations but also their performance (Duverger 1963; Harmel and Janda 1982; von Beyme 1985; Powell 1982). Nonetheless, there is no agreement on their impact on party organizations.

In arguing for both the importance of the electoral rules and the positive impact of proportional representation systems on the development of party organization, Duverger maintains that

> the list vote (scrutin de liste), operating within the framework of a large constituency, obliges the caucuses or local branches of the party to establish amongst themselves a strong system of articulation within the constituency, so that they can agree upon the composition of the lists. On the other hand, the single-member system (scrutin uninominal), operating in a small constituency, tends to make each small local group of the party into an independent entity, and consequently weaken the articulation of the party (1963, 45 emphasis in original).

It follows from Duverger's assertion that countries with proportional representation systems will tend to have more complex organizations vis-a-vis single-member plurality systems where party organizations tend to be weaker and campaigns are more candidate-centered as in the United States.

However, von Beyme (1985) argues from a totally opposite perspective by contending that

> parties in systems with a plurality vote have developed strong constituency organizations...In democracies with a proportional election system, on the other hand, the constituencies are too big to form basic units. In some countries the conferences of constituency delegates are more of the nature of single-purpose meetings and they do not do the continuous work a constituency unit does in Britain or the USA (the Federal Republic of Germany is one example of this) (1985, 189).

From both Blondel's and von Beyme's arguments it is not possible to determine which perspective is correct. Nonetheless, in an empirical examination of the impact of electoral system on party organization, Harmel and Janda (1982) found support for Duverger's arguments, i.e., the more proportional the electoral rules the more complex the party organization. The empirical analysis to be undertaken here permits us to "stack up" evidence for or against Blondel's or von Beyme's hypotheses.

Size of the Country

Whether a country is geographically large or small is often said to affect distribution of power between a political party's national organ and the local organs. Blondel (1969), for instance, argued that "the greater the distance between the centre and the periphery, the more centralized rule is to be avoided; as a result, a large or populous country is less likely to be centralized than a small or scarcely populated polity" (Blondel 1969, 285).

While Blondel simply states a proposition, Harmel and Janda explain the logic behind the need for more decentralized rule in a country with larger size. They argue that

> the sheer impracticality of trying to be the eyes and ears to the entire dispersed population has often become a burden for which both the leaders and the citizens of large nations have welcomed more localized governmental bodies with the power and the responsibility to make decisions on local issues. Likewise, political parties may conclude that local party organs are better suited than the national level to making decisions concerning local issues and localized party activities (1982, 63).

These discussions in the literature lead us to expect that there will be a direct and positive relationship between country size and centralization of power. That is, the greater the country size the more centralized the power.

Size of the Population

One other system-level factor that is said to affect the complexity of the party organization is the population size of the country. In a study of state social service agencies, Blau and Schoenherr (1971) observed that a state's population size affects the division of labor and the hierarchical levels within the agency. Similarly, Blondel (1969) argued that whether political parties extend their "tentacles" is affected by the size of the population. Harmel and Janda (1982, 50) found that population size is positively related to the complexity of party organization. From these discussions then, we should expect that the greater the population size the greater the organizational complexity.

Summary

In the discussion above I have identified from the literature some relevant system-level determinants of party organization attributes and performance and how they affect the party. One may ask: Are these the only relevant environmental variables affecting party organization and performance? Harmel and Janda (1982) have identified numerous system-level variables that influence how a party organizes. However, in that particular study they are examining a broader sample of political parties from around the world.[6] By sampling a wider spectrum of political parties inclusion of many relevant systemic factors is logical.[7] In this particular study, I have purposely limited the area of examination to only include several Western industrialized democracies due to availability of quantitative data. It is important to note, however, that because of the restriction of the geographical area in the empirical examination many environmental variables are already effectively controlled for.

For this reason, I have not included some of the environmental factors (e.g. modernization, extent of suffrage) that have already been identified in the literature as having a bearing on the party organizations and performance. Nonetheless, the environmental factors I use as control variables have been identified in earlier work as among the most important determinants of organizational attributes and performance. In the following chapter, the hypotheses proposed in this chapter will be empirically tested using data obtained from both Janda's International Comparative Political Parties project and Katz and Mair's Party Organizations project.

Notes

1. Organizational complexity encompasses "the division of labor, formalization of rules, impersonality of relationships, and forms of role and structural differentiation of the organization" (Harmel and Janda 1982, 43). Simply put, the more elaborate the structure, the more complex the party organization.

2. In their study of formal organizations in general, Blau and Schoenherr (1971, 301) propose that "increasing size generates structural differentiation in organization" (1971, 301). Tomasko asserts that "(b)ig seems to breed bigger," that is, big membership leads to bigger organizational structure (1987, 14).

3. It is interesting to note at first glance, however, that corporations and agencies are comparatively smaller than political parties. The size of the organizations included in the studies cited are smaller than the smallest political party. Nonetheless, it is important to distinguish that there is a qualitative difference between the employees of an agency or business and the members of a political party. Whereas employees of corporations may be full-time workers, most political party members may only be involved part-time. Within political parties, the ordinary members can be distinguished from the militants by their level of participation (Duverger 1963).

4. In a sense this is the confusion that Blondel introduces when he uses the term decentralization to mean administrative decentralization.

5. Harmel and Janda (1982) distinguish between "centralization of power" as denoting the relationship between the layers of the organization and "concentration of power" as the horizontal relationship involving the number of people making effective decisions (see also Harmel 1989).

6. This study of environmental effects on party characteristics examines 95 political parties operating during 1957 to 1962 in 28 countries. These parties represent many regions of the world including Anglo-America, West Europe, Scandinavia and the Lowlands, South and Central America, Asia and the Far East, Africa and the Middle East.

7. Some of the environmental factors I excluded are: modernity, restriction on suffrage, recency of democratic experience, separation of powers, parliamentary vs. presidential systems.

3   Empirical Tests of the Cross-sectional Model

In order to properly test the hypotheses set forth in the preceding chapter, it is essential to have good cross-sectional data and appropriate methodology. In this chapter, I will describe the data set that is used in testing the cross-sectional hypotheses and the methodology used to empirically test them.

Data

Janda defines political parties as "organizations that pursue a goal of placing their avowed representatives in government positions" (1980, 5). Placement of representatives in government office can encompasses various strategies, e.g., subverting the political system or joining elections. Nonetheless, for the purposes of this study, it is important to determine whether the political parties included are to some extent electorally motivated.

In the International Comparative Political Parties (ICPP) project, Janda (1980) included both legal and illegal parties in the data set which are identified as having some importance in national politics. In the case of the legal parties, the political parties have to win "at least 5 percent of the seats in the lower house of the national legislature in two or more successive elections" (Janda 1980, 7). Hence, given that they were all included in the ICPP data set, the political parties included in this study have at one time or another participated in elections and have won at least five percent of the votes in the successive elections covered in the period 1950-1962.[1]

To test the cross-sectional model, this study will use the ICPP data that cover several Western industrial democracies from the period 1950-1962, as well as data from Katz and Mair's data set, which covers seven Western democracies from 1960 to 1989. Political parties to be included in this part of the study are 37 political parties from Australia (2), Austria (3), Canada (4), Denmark (4), Germany (3), Iceland (4), Ireland (3), New Zealand (2), Netherlands (6), Sweden (4), and the United Kingdom (2).

Appendix I presents a list of the specific political parties and countries included in this study. All the countries and parties cited above were included in the ICPP project conducted by Kenneth Janda. While the test of the cross-sectional model will involve examining the period from 1957-1962,[2] the longitudinal analysis of Chapter Five will cover the whole period from 1960-1990, for a subset of these parties. As in Katz and Mair, France is not included in this dissertation since "there has been a marked lack of party organizational continuity in the period" concerned (1992, viii). Greece (also Spain and Portugal), on the other hand, was excluded since "democracy was only relatively recently re-established" (Katz and Mair 1992, viii).

In operationalizing the variables, this study will be relying on both the Janda (1980) and Katz and Mair (1992) data sets. It is important to note that the ICPP data set consists of judgemental data based on review of the secondary literature, while the Katz and Mair data set is based on review of official party records.

The operationalization adopted for the main independent variable, party membership size, will be the average number of direct individual members of the political party from 1960 to 1962, with data coming from the Katz and Mair data set for all countries except Australia, Canada, Iceland, and New Zealand.[3] The membership figure for the Australian Labor Party is obtained from Warhurst's (1983) study, the figure for the New Zealand Labour Party is obtained from Webber (1978), and the membership figure for Australian Liberal Party is provided by Alistair Kinloch.[4]

This operational decision is not as clearcut or non-controversial as some might think. In the complex organization literature there exists a healthy debate about what is the appropriate measurement of organization size. Most of these debates center on whether size should be measured as the clientele served by the organization, the number of employees of the organization, or the volume of business that the organization transacts (e.g. sales) (Blau 1970; Blau and Schoenherr 1971; Ford 1980a). Within the study of political parties, parallel issues have been discussed such as whether the size of a political party should be measured as the ratio of members in the electorate, or should be measured on the basis of number of votes or supporters, or should include the members of ancillary organizations and corporate or union members as well as direct members (Widfeldt 1992; Smith 1991).

While the merit of this debate lies in furthering conceptual clarification of political party size, the focus of this study is on one particular dimension of size. This study is primarily concerned with the internal aspects and features of the political party itself and the consequent impact of party membership size on other attributes of the organization. Widfeldt suggests that "direct membership is the most straightforward (or least roundabout) way of describing the membership size of a party" (1992, 9). In this study, I operationalize party membership size as the size of direct membership. Although this operationalization is not devoid of problems, using direct membership and excluding indirect membership helps to avoid the problem of overestimating party membership.

For one of the dependent variables, organizational complexity, we adopt Janda's definition of the degree of organization as "the complexity of regularized procedures for mobilizing and coordinating the efforts of party supporters in executing the party's strategy and tactics" (1980, 98). Using this definition, organizational complexity encompasses the formalization of procedures and structural differentiation of the organization (Harmel and Janda 1982). In this sense, the more elaborate the political party structure, the more complex the organization is.

Organizational complexity of the political party is measured in this study using the seven indicators provided in the International Comparative Parties Project of Kenneth Janda:

1. Structural articulation - scored from 0 to 11, this indicator is concerned with how well-defined are the party organs and how clear are the functional relationships of these organs. Higher scores are given when numerous national organs have clear functional responsibilities.
2. Intensiveness of organization - scored from 0 to 6, this indicator measures how small is the basic element of the political party. The higher score is given when the party's basic units is relatively small.
3. Extensiveness of organization - scored from 0 to 6, this indicator measures the geographical coverage of the political party organization. The higher score is given when the country is thoroughly covered by party units.
4. Frequency of local meetings - scored from 0 to 3, this indicator measures the regularity of meetings at the local level. The higher score is given when local party meetings are frequent.
5. Frequency of national meetings - scored from 0 to 6, this

indicator measures the regularity of meetings at the national level. The higher score is given when national party meetings are frequent.

6. Maintaining records - scored from 0 to 16, this indicator measures whether the party maintains a list of party members, has a publishing program, a research division or a party archive. The higher score is given when the party has a research division or archive, publishing program, and maintains quality membership lists.

7. Pervasiveness of organization - scored from 0 to 18, this indicator measures the "party penetration into mass social and economic groups representing politically significant sectors of the population" (Janda 1980, 105). The higher score is given when the party penetrates numerous socioeconomic sectors and has many adherents.

For the "centralization of power" variable, the study will also utilize the indicators developed in the International Comparative Political Parties project to operationalize the variable. This variable mainly taps the "location and distribution of effective decision-making authority within the party" (Janda 1980, 108). We are concerned here with how the local party organs relate to the national party organs as far as effective decision-making authority is concerned, that is, the vertical dimension of intra-organizational relations. The seven indicators of centralization of power are as follows:

1. Nationalization of structure - scored from 0 to 6, this indicator measures the strength of national committee control of the party. The higher score is given when there is a hierarchical structure with the national level organ in ultimate control.

2. Selection of national leader - scored from 0 to 8, this indicator measures the procedures used by the party to select its national leader. The higher score is given to parties in which ultimate selection power resides in the national organs.

3. Selection of parliamentary candidates - scored from 1 to 9, this indicator measures the distribution of control over the selection of candidates for the legislature. The higher score is given when the selection is done by the national organ.

4. Allocation of funds - scored from 0 to 6, this indicator measures the control of funds collection and allocation within the party. The higher score is given when the national organ collects and allocates party funds.
5. Formulation of policy - scored from 0 to 7, this indicator measures where the power lies concerning determination of party policy. The higher score given when major policy positions are determined by the party leader and/or a small subgroup of the national organ.
6. Control of communications - scored from 0 to 7, this indicator measures where the level of the party that controls the content and distribution of its party publications and media. The higher score is given when the national organ controls its own media.
7. Administration of discipline - scored from 0 to 4, this indicator measures the location of power as far as administering rewards or punishment is concerned. The higher score is given when the national organ administers major disciplinary techniques.

Regarding concentration of power, the ICPP data set provides an indicator of leadership concentration. This indicator basically refers "to the number of individuals who constitute the top party hierarchy and who are regarded as key decision makers within the party" (Janda 1980, 116). This indicator is scored from 0 to 6 with the low score given when the leadership is so dispersed that only regional leaders can be identified and the high score given when a single leader exercises all the power.

For the intra-party democratic performance variable, this study will only utilize one indicator of involvement found in the ICPP project. Since we are concerned primarily with the level of participation rather than the incentives that motivate the participation of members, the best indicator of this would be the degrees of participation of members. In the ICPP project, membership participation is measured on a scale from 0 to 6 with the low score given if members are only nominal and the high score given if most members conscientiously attend party activities.

With regards to the system level variables, we relied on Blondel's (1969) *Introduction to Comparative Government* and Russett et al's (1964) *World Handbook of Political and Social Indicators* for the data.[5] I use the data provided for area size and population size in the *World Handbook*. Area size is measured in square kilometers while population is the population as of 1961. In the case of formal federalism, I adopted the approach of Blondel (1969), who simply dichotomized the structure of the state into unitary or federal, where "1" is assigned to a unitary state and "2" to a federal state.[6]

For electoral system, I chose to use Blondel's (1969) continuum of electoral systems that is measured from less proportional to more proportional. Electoral system is coded as "1" when the country is only one constituency and it is fully proportional representation and coded as "6" when the electoral system used is a one ballot majority system and the whole country is one constituency.[7] It is more desirable to measure the degree of proportionality, than to use a simple dichotomy, since the range of electoral systems is more complex than simply dichotomizing between a proportional representation system on the one hand and majority/plurality system on the other.[8]

Since the variables organization complexity and centralization of power are measured by multiple indicators with varying scales, simple averaging of these scores on these indicators to create an index inappropriately weights the impact of the indicators on a particular index. To avoid the problem of inappropriately weighing the indicators included in the indices, the summated z-scoring technique is employed as in Harmel and Janda (1982).[9] An average composite score for organizational complexity was computed for each party in the sample;[10] the higher the score on the average composite score for organizational complexity, the more complex the political party. The range of the organizational complexity scores derived from the calculations described above ranges from a low score of -1.467, which is the Canadian Social Credit Party, and a high score of 1.105, for the German Social Democratic Party (SPD). Table 3.1 shows the 37 political parties and their average composite score on organizational complexity.

In the case of the variable "centralization of power," the above procedure employed in calculating the average composite score was replicated, the higher the average composite score for this variable the more centralized the political party. The scores for centralization of power range from a low of -1.26, which is for the Swedish Liberal party, to a high score of 1.07, for the Dutch Communist Party. Table 3.2 shows the 37 political parties and their average composite score in centralization of power.

Table 3.1   Organizational Complexity Scores

Country	Party	Average Composite Score
Australia	Labor Party	-0.24
	Liberal Party	-0.59
Austria	Austrian People's Party	0.765
	Socialist Party	0.366
	Freedom Party	-1.09
Canada	Conservative Party	-0.397
	Liberal Party	-0.357
	New Democratic Party	0.253
	Social Credit Party	-1.467
Denmark	Social Democratic Party	0.000
	Liberal Party	0.086
	Conservative People's Party	0.449
	Social Liberal Party	-0.03
Germany	Christian Democratic Union	0.719
	Free Democratic Party	0.000
	Social Democratic Party	1.105
Iceland	Independence Party	-0.404
	Progressive Party	-0.213
	People's Alliance	0.419
	Social Democratic Party	-0.823
Ireland	Fianna Fail	-0.542
	Fine Gael	-0.553
	Labour Party	-0.840
Netherlands	Dutch Communist Party	0.439
	Labour Party	0.607
	Anti-Revolutionary Party	0.549
	Christian Historical Union	-0.33
	Catholic People's Party	-0.060
	Liberal Party	-0.026
New Zealand	National Party	-0.385
	Labour Party	0.417
Sweden	Social Democratic Party	0.822
	Center Party	0.303
	People's Party	-0.55
	Moderate Party	-0.52
U.K.	Conservative Party	0.366
	Labour Party	0.242

Table 3.2 **Centralization of Power Scores**

Country	Party	Average Composite Score
Australia	Labor Party	-0.48
	Liberal Party	-0.64
Austria	Austrian People's Party	-0.15
	Socialist Party	0.443
	Freedom Party	0.319
Canada	Conservative Party	-0.191
	Liberal Party	-0.424
	New Democratic Party	-0.492
	Social Credit Party	-0.780
Denmark	Social Democratic Party	0.376
	Liberal Party	0.528
	Conservative People's Party	0.528
	Social Liberal Party	0.447
Germany	Christian Democratic Union	0.092
	Free Democratic Party	0.096
	Social Democratic Party	-0.25
Iceland	Independence Party	0.934
	Progressive Party	0.40
	People's Alliance	1.015
	Social Democratic Party	0.915
Ireland	Fianna Fail	0.709
	Fine Gael	0.082
	Labour Party	0.384
Netherlands	Dutch Communist Party	1.079
	Labour Party	-0.01
	Anti-Revolutionary Party	0.039
	Christian Historical Union	-0.33
	Catholic People's Party	-0.23
	Liberal Party	-0.46
New Zealand	National Party	-0.255
	Labour Party	0.041
Sweden	Social Democratic Party	-0.65
	Center Party	-1.23
	People's Party	-1.27
	Moderate Party	-0.94
U.K.	Conservative Party	0.595
	Labour Party	0.533

Table 3.3 Concentration of Power Scores

Country	Party	Average Composite Score
Australia	Labor Party	-0.25
	Liberal Party	-1.40
Austria	Austrian People's Party	0.318
	Socialist Party	0.890
	Freedom Party	0.890
Canada	Conservative Party	2.03
	Liberal Party	0.318
	New Democratic Party	0.318
	Social Credit Party	-0.254
Denmark	Social Democratic Party	0.318
	Liberal Party	0.318
	Conservative People's Party	0.318
	Social Liberal Party	0.318
Germany	Christian Democratic Union	0.890
	Free Democratic Party	-0.25
	Social Democratic Party	0.890
Iceland	Independence Party	0.318
	Progressive Party	0.318
	People's Alliance	0.318
	Social Democratic Party	0.318
Ireland	Fianna Fail	0.89
	Fine Gael	0.89
	Labour Party	0.00
Netherlands	Dutch Communist Party	0.89
	Labour Party	-1.40
	Anti-Revolutionary Party	-1.40
	Christian Historical Union	-1.40
	Catholic People's Party	-1.40
	Liberal Party	-1.40
New Zealand	National Party	0.318
	Labour Party	0.318
Sweden	Social Democratic Party	-1.40
	Center Party	-1.40
	People's Party	-1.40
	Moderate Party	-1.40
U.K.	Conservative Party	2.035
	Labour Party	0.318

Table 3.4   Intra-party Democratic Performance Scores

Country	Party	Average Composite Score
Australia	Labor Party	1.190
	Liberal Party	0.000
Austria	Austrian People's Party	-0.73
	Socialist Party	1.190
	Freedom Party	0.000
Canada	Conservative Party	0.00
	Liberal Party	0.00
	New Democratic Party	0.00
	Social Credit Party	0.00
Denmark	Social Democratic Party	0.228
	Liberal Party	0.228
	Conservative People's Party	0.228
	Social Liberal Party	0.228
Germany	Christian Democratic Union	1.186
	Free Democratic Party	0.000
	Social Democratic Party	2.140
Iceland	Independence Party	0.00
	Progressive Party	0.00
	People's Alliance	0.00
	Social Democratic Party	0.00
Ireland	Fianna Fail	0.00
	Fine Gael	0.00
	Labour Party	0.00
Netherlands	Dutch Communist Party	0.00
	Labour Party	0.228
	Anti-Revolutionary Party	0.228
	Christian Historical Union	0.228
	Catholic People's Party	-1.69
	Liberal Party	-1.69
New Zealand	National Party	0.00
	Labour Party	-0.73
Sweden	Social Democratic Party	0.228
	Center Party	-0.73
	People's Party	0.228
	Moderate Party	0.228
U.K.	Conservative Party	-1.69
	Labour Party	-0.73

The variable "concentration of power" was also standardized using the summated z-scoring technique and as with the other variables, the higher the score the greater the concentration of power.[11] The scores for concentration of power ranges from low scores of -1.399 for several political parties, e.g., Dutch Catholic People's Party and Liberal Party of Australia, and high score of 2.035 for the British Conservative Party. Table 3.3 shows the 37 political parties and their respective score on concentration of power.

The democratic participation variable was also standardized by using the z-scoring technique; as in the above variables the higher the score the greater the level of participation. In our sample of 37 political parties, the range of democratic participation scores is from a high of 2.14 for the SPD to a low score of -1.687 for the Dutch Catholic People's Party, the Dutch Liberal Party and the British Labour Party. Table 3.4 shows the 37 political parties and their scores on intra-party participation.

Research Design and Empirical Tests

Harmel (1989) suggests that Michels' theory has neglected to account for the influences of the environment on the political party. In this study small sample size and the limited information on some political parties will prevent the use of a dummy variable to account for country effects on each political party. In order to control for the effects of system level factors on the political party, I identified some system level variables that are suggested in the literature as having significant impact on how political parties organize (see Harmel and Janda 1982).

Ordinary least squares regression was employed to empirically test the hypotheses set forth in the previous chapter. The ordinary least squares regression was supplemented by a number of diagnostic tests. Because of the small sample size and to ensure that the results are not unduly influenced by outliers or discrepant observations, several diagnostic checks were used. There are several statistics that help detect influential observations, for this study I chose to use studentized residuals. A particular observation is considered influential when the studentized residuals have an absolute value greater than 2.0. The results of these tests are reported in the following section.

Results

The first hypothesis posits a curvilinear relationship between party size and organizational complexity. After taking the natural log of party membership size, ordinary least squares regression was used. The regression results, provided in Table 3.5, indicate that size significantly predicts a political party's organizational complexity.[12] As in the studies of other types of complex organizations, the results suggest that as party size increases, organizational complexity increases in a curvilinear fashion.

Table 3.5   Regression Results of Organizational Complexity

	All observations	Excluding influentials[a]
Constant	-3.8235**	-5.396***
	(1.567)	(1.584)
Party size (log)	0.31937***	0.33179***
	(0.08127)	(0.0741)
Electoral system	-0.17872**	-0.3113***
	(0.1028)	(0.1101)
Population (log)	0.03121	0.13348
	(0.0991)	(0.1007)
R-squared	0.47	0.58
Adjusted R-squared	0.40	0.52
N	24	23[b]

Note: Entries are unstandardized regression coefficients. Standard errors are in parentheses.
*$p<.10$ (one-tailed); **$p<.05$ (one-tailed); ***$p<.01$ (one-tailed)
[a]Influential observations are observations that are outliers and "observations that have a strong influence on the OLS estimates" (Kennedy 1992, 280).
[b]New Zealand Labour Party is excluded because the studentized residual is greater than 2.0.

Harmel and Janda (1982) suggested system level variables such as the size of the population and the type of electoral system significantly affect organizational complexity. In order to control for the effects of the systemic factors these were included in our ordinary least squares equation. The results indicate that electoral system is a statistically significant factor influencing party organizational complexity.[13] As in Harmel and Janda

(1982), it is evident that the more proportional the electoral system, the greater the need for complex party organization. The findings also show that controlling for the effects of system level variables does not diminish the impact of party membership size on organizational complexity.

The finding that party membership size is a significant factor affecting party complexity is important in light of the fact that system level variables are generally given more prominence in the explanation of how parties organize. At an intuitive level it can be argued that parties do not organize only in response to the pressure of their environments but internal factors (primarily party membership size) may also create pressure on political parties to attempt to resolve problems arising from the growth in organizational size. In other words, parties decide to be more organizationally complex not only in response to the environment but also to address practical issues of efficiently and effectively organizing their members.

On the impact of organizational complexity and the centralization of power, Michels contends that the development of the organization inevitably leads to the fundamental alteration of the distribution of power within the political party. He argues that "the increase in the power of the leaders is directly proportional with the extension of the organization" (Michels 1962, 71). The test of a derivation of this argument does not provide support for the hypothesis that organizational complexity leads to more centralization of power after controlling for the impact of geographical size and formal federalism (see Table 3.6).

In fact there is no indication that a complex organization necessarily leads to centralization of power (see also Harmel 1989). The Austrian People's Party (OVP) is a case in point. While it is among the most organized of the political parties included in the sample it is also one of the most decentralized. The decentralization of power within the OVP is the result of the nature of how the party is organized. The OVP is basically split into three main leagues which to a certain extent keeps the leagues' own power base intact (Muller and Steininger 1994). As a result, the national executive is comparatively weaker at least in the method that centralization of power is operationalized in this study.[14]

The German Social Democratic Party (SPD), which Michels wrote about in formulating his Iron Law of Oligarchy, is very highly organized but is not as centralized as many other political parties in the sample. In comparing the British Labour Party and the SPD, Thomas Koelble described the Labour Party as "comparatively decentralized since it affords decision-making power to an organization outside of the party which is very decentralized in itself" (1991, 42). While this may be true in the Labour Party of the 1980s, the Labour Party of the 1950s is characterized more by numerous observers as governed by the principle of democratic centralism (Shaw 1988). Hence, the centralization of power score for the Labour Party in this study is higher than the SPD's.

Table 3.6   Regression Results of Centralization of Power

	All observations
Constant	-0.09338
	(1.364)
Complexity	-0.09
	(0.2576)
Party size (log)	0.16427*
	(0.1104)
Area (log)	-0.22462***
	(0.07316)
Federalism	0.40513**
	(0.2287)
R-squared	0.39
Adjusted R-squared	0.26
N	24

Note: Entries are unstandardized regression coefficients. Standard errors are in parentheses.
*$p<.10$ (one-tailed); **$p<.05$ (one-tailed); ***$p<.01$ (one-tailed)

Blondel contends that as "parties grow in size and complexity, the relationship between the top and bottom of the hierarchy also becomes more complex" (1978, 148). Sub-leaders in charge of local and regional offices are needed in order to "organize and supervise large numbers of small groups" (Blondel 1978, 148). According to Blondel, then, sub-leaders gain autonomy and authority that eventually contributes to the decentralized character of the party.[15]

The results in Table 3.6 cannot confirm the effect of increasing complexity on (de)centralization as Blondel has argued (see Harmel 1989).

However, the results show instead that party size affects centralization of power; i.e., the larger the party size the greater the centralization of power. It is interesting to note that while hypothesis 2a calls for a direct relationship between organizational complexity and centralization of power, the estimated coefficient bears a negative sign. This result may give some credence to Blondel's argument of increasing complexity leading to decreasing centralization of power.

Table 3.7 **Regression Results of Concentration of Power**

	All observations	Excluding influentials
Constant	-5.1382**	-1.9821
	(2.591)	(2.758)
Complexity	-0.36327	-0.03009
	(0.4894)	(0.4707)
Party size (log)	0.50295**	0.21485
	(0.2098)	(0.2313)
Area (log)	-0.21801*	-0.21922**
	(0.1390)	(0.1266)
Federalism	1.1065***	1.2404***
	(0.4345)	(0.4005)
R-squared	0.40	0.40
Adjusted R-squared	0.27	0.26
N	24	23[a]

Note: Entries are unstandardized regression coefficients. Standard errors are in parentheses.
*$p<.10$ (one-tailed); **$p<.05$ (one-tailed); ***$p<.01$ (one-tailed)
[a]British Conservative Party is excluded because studentized residual is greater than 2.0.

Centralization of power mainly relates to the "distribution of control over decision making among the levels of party organization" (Harmel and Janda 1982, 59). In other words, it is the "extent to which the national level of party organization is free from control by the regional and the local levels in conducting what would normally be considered national party business and is capable of enforcing its decisions on the subnational organs" (Harmel and Janda 1982, 59-60). In this usage, centralization of power is distinguished from concentration of power which refers to the "control of national-level organs by one or more national-level leaders" (Harmel and Janda 1982, 72). That is, centralization of power pertains to the vertical relationship between national organs and lower levels of organization, while concentration of power pertains to the horizontal relationship of how many individuals participate in national party-decision making.

Michels (1962) asserts that large political parties are able to combine organizational complexity and oligarchical power. Moreover, Panebianco (1988) suggests that increasing party organizational complexity does not necessarily lead to a dispersion of authority. These arguments lead us to expect a direct relationship between organizational complexity, party size and concentration of power. On this horizontal dimension of power, the results of the empirical tests show that after controlling for the effects of system level factors and the impact of influential observations, neither organizational complexity nor party size is a statistically significant predictor of concentration of power (see Table 3.7).

With regards to the effect of systemic-level factors, the results contained in Tables 3.6 and 3.7 show that both size of a country and formal federalism are statistically related to centralization and concentration of power. In the case of country size, the results show that the larger the country the more decentralized the political party. As Harmel and Janda explain

> the sheer impracticality of trying to be the eyes and ears to the entire dispersed population has often become a burden for which both the leaders and citizens of large nations have welcomed more localized governmental bodies with the power and the responsibility to make decisions on local issues. Likewise, political parties may conclude that local party organs are better suited than the national level to making decisions concerning local issues and localized party activities (1982, 63).

Blondel argues that "federal countries are also those in which the parties' State or provincial organs are strongest" (1978, 151). The tendency of federal countries in breeding more decentralized parties is basically a consequence of the institutional designs of these countries. According to Blondel, a federal governmental structure leads to decentralization of political parties because it increases the number of positions that parties can compete for. As a result, "politicians are therefore more likely to want positions at State or provincial level; and parties are correspondingly involved" (Blondel 1978, 151). From these arguments, we should expect that federalism should be inversely related to both centralization and concentration of power.

The findings of this study, however, contradict the arguments just presented. That is, my findings indicate that formal federalism contributes to more centralization and concentration of party power. This counter-theoretical findings may be explained by the fact that if there is no actual decentralization of power in the polity, simply the existence of formal federal structure will not require political parties to decentralize power (see also Harmel and Janda 1982, 69).[16] Interestingly, with regards to centralization of power and concentration of power in political parties, we can infer from the results of the empirical tests that environmental factors or system level variables play a consistently more important role in the distribution of power within the parties.

Michels declares that the advance of party organization necessarily results in the decline of intra-party democracy. Our fourth hypothesis, derived from Michels, leads us to expect an inverse relationship between organizational complexity and party democratic performance. The results of the regression analysis are presented in Table 3.8.

The results of the multivariate analysis show that the level of intra-party democratic performance or participation and organizational complexity is statistically significant at the 0.05 level. It is interesting to note that the results obtained is the reverse of that posited in hypothesis 4. In fact, the results in Table 3.8 show that the more complex a party organization is, the higher the level of intra-party democracy or participation. However, our analysis also shows that party size is not statistically related to the level of participation in the political party, and in fact the sign of the estimated coefficient is in the wrong direction from that expected.

From the results in Table 3.5 we know that party size relates to organizational complexity, and likewise party size theoretically attenuates the level of participation. However, Table 3.8 also tells us that the more organizationally complex the party is the greater the level of participation. How can these findings be explained? On the reverse findings regarding complexity and participation, an intuitive explanation could be the fact that the more complex a party organization the more opportunities there are for party members to participate in party activities. Crotty (1971) suggested that organization matters as far as providing the avenues for more party activities. In this context therefore, it is logical to argue that more party activities means more chances for participation.

Table 3.8   Regression Results of Intra-party Participation

	All observations	Excluding influentials
Constant	1.9340	4.6057*
	(3.806)	(3.217)
Complexity	0.64717*	0.84813**
	(0.4737)	(0.3909)
Party size (log)	-0.10975	-0.21038
	(0.2092)	(0.1847)
Population (log)	-0.10975	-0.21261
	(0.2288)	(0.2043)
Area (log)	0.068193	-0.02275
	(0.1342)	(0.1131)
Federalism	0.91002**	1.2615***
	(0.4431)	(0.4157)
R-squared	0.3112	0.5018
Adjusted R-squared	0.1198	0.3461
N	24	22[a]

Note: Entries are unstandardized regression coefficients. Standard errors are in parentheses.
*$p<.10$ (one-tailed); **$p<.05$ (one-tailed); ***$p<.01$ (one-tailed)
[a]Austrian People's Party and Dutch Liberal Party are excluded because their studentized residuals are greater than 2.0.

Yet, another explanation for these "anomalous" findings may come from the logic of collective action as proposed by Mancur Olson (1965). While large party size has (at least in theory) a dampening effect on member participation, growth in size leads to the rise of organization. In political parties, the growth of organizations implies that political parties may organize at lower levels as in the precincts or even the cells as found in communist parties. Consequently, the smaller size of these lower level organizations facilitates participation rather than impeding it. Unlike Blondel, Michels fails to foresee that the development of complex organizations and hierarchies resulting from increasing party size actually provides more opportunities for membership participation. Indeed in a path analytic analysis of the impacts of party membership size (without controls for system-level variables), Tan (1998) finds that party membership size has both a direct and indirect effect on a party's level of intra-party democratic performance. Party membership size has a negative direct effect on the level of intra-party democratic performance, i.e., it dampens intra-party democratic performance. On the other hand, party membership size has a positive indirect effect on intra-party democratic performance by stimulating the growth of complex organization.

Summary

Does party size affect organizational complexity? Do party size and organizational complexity impact on party electoral and democratic performance and other organizational attributes? These are the key questions posed in the earlier chapters of this study.

From the analysis of available cross-sectional data we can conclude that party size does affect party complexity, electoral performance, and centralization of power, even with controls for system level factors. However, the findings of the tests of the cross-sectional model do not support the arguments that organizational complexity affects other organizational attributes and performance (except for intra-party participation).

The important point to keep in mind from the findings presented in this chapter is that it indicates the critical party level variables influencing organizational structure and norms. Moreover, the findings provide a starting point to examine the relationships of these attributes in a dynamic setting particularly in an era of party size decline in Western democracies. Since party size is critical in determining organizational arrangements and performance, it is important to examine the implications of the decline in party size (membership) on organizational attributes and performance over time. More importantly the critical question that needs to be asked is: What is the impact of *declining* party size on a political party's intra-party democratic performance? This will be the main focus of the following chapters of this study.

Notes

1. Political parties that won five percent of the votes after the cut-off year of 1962 are excluded from Janda's ICPP data set. Those parties are, however, mentioned in the data set but no data are provided.

2. Janda's ICPP data set covers the period 1950-1962. These twelve years were divided into 1950-1956 and 1957-1962. Instead of providing annual data for each variable, average scores for each six-year half are provided. As an illustration, each political party is given a score for the period 1950-1956 on its 'frequency of national meetings' (an indicator of organizational complexity) and another score for the period 1957-1962 if it is different from the earlier period. Since Katz and Mai's data covers 1960-1990, only the 1957-1962 data from Janda's ICPP project will be used for the analysis of the cross-sectional model since there is at least some overlap in time period of the two data sets.

3. Of the 37 political parties in the sample, 13 parties do not have available party membership figures. Parties without party membership figures include the 3 parties from Ireland, 4 parties from Canada, 4 parties from Iceland, 1 each from the Netherlands, and New Zealand. Although included in the Katz and Mair data set the 3 Irish parties, and the Communist Party of the Netherlands do not have membership figures reported for the period covered in this study. The membership figure for the German FDP is an estimate given in Mair (1994). Membership figures for the New Zealand National Party are unavailable since the party headquarters cannot provide this information because it is "contravening the Rules of the Party" (personal correspondence with Margaret Skews, New Zealand National Party executive director March 19, 1995).

4. Alistair Kinloch, Australian Liberal Party Manager for Policy and Parliamentary Affairs, provided an estimate of their membership figure (personal correspondence, March 21, 1995).

5. It is important to note that the main difference between this study and the Harmel and Janda (1982) study is that the cases used for this study are restricted to Western industrial democracies while the Harmel and Janda study included all types of party systems. Since the data used here are similar to the Harmel and Janda (1982) study, it is not surprising that many of the empirical findings should be similar between the two studies.

6. In this study, we tap only one dimension of decentralization of state power - formal federalism. The older dimension, effective decentralization, is not tapped in this study (see Harmel and Janda 1982, 65-66, for detailed discussion about effective/actual decentralization versus formal federalism).

7. Blondel's (1969, 534) 6-point coding of electoral system is as follows:
   1. Fully proportional representation; only one constituency.
   2. Proportional representation within constituencies.
   3. Alternative vote; 2-ballot; limited vote.
   4. Single-member majority system, one ballot.
   5. Multi-member majority system, one ballot.

6. One ballot majority system and the whole country as one constituency.

8. Further refinements to Blondel's simple continuum can be made to include indicators such as deviation to proportionality which can capture the effects of the varying electoral formulas adopted by different countries.

9. Rather than arbitrarily giving unequal weights to the seven indicators in the construction of the index, the summated z-scoring technique gives equal weights to all indicators.

10. In constructing a composite score for the variables the means and standard deviations of each of the seven indicators were calculated. These were then use to calculate the z-scores of each indicator for each of the 37 political parties in the sample. The z-scores of each of the seven indicators were then summated across all seven indicators. An average composite was then derived by dividing by the number of indicators on when the party has a score (adjusting for missing information).

11. Although this is not a multiple indicator variable, I have chosen to use summated z-scores in the empirical tests. Using z-scores or the raw scores for this particular variable should not affect the ranking of the parties on this variable and more importantly on the results of the empirical tests.

12. For this and all other results reported, I performed the usual diagnostics. Due to the small sample size, I was particularly concerned with the possibility that the results might be affected by one or a few influential cases. To test, I relied on the inspection of studentized residuals. In a few instances there were some mildly suspicious cases (studentized residuals greater than 2.0). In order to account for these influential observations, I ran OLS regression without these observations. The results of these "sanitized" regression are provided for comparison. In most instances, omitting the suspicious observation does not change the estimates of concern to this study appreciably.

13. Since the data used here are the same as in Harmel and Janda (1982) except for the more restricted number of political parties included in the sample, the empirical findings of the Harmel and Janda (1982) study are expected to remain the same.

14. For details of OVP's numerous failed attempts to transform itself to an effectively centralized party, see Muller and Steininger 1994.

15. For arguments about organizational complexity and decentralization applied to organizations other than political parties, see Prechel 1991 and references in the article.

16. There is reason to believe that the size of a country and formal federalism may be related, i.e., the greater the size the more likely the country is to adopt a federal form of government. To check if size of the country can significantly predict formal federalism, I regress formal federalism on the size of the country (log). The result of this inquiry shows that size of the country is directly related to formal federalism and the relationship is statistically significant at the 0.05 level. Statistically, even with the collinearity problem of the variables "formal federalism" and "size of country," OLS estimates remain the best linear unbiased estimators

(Kennedy 1992, 177). However, collinearity may result in inflated standard errors and low t-statistics for the independent variables that are collinear. That is, we are more likely not to reject a false null hypothesis (Type II error) with respect to the estimated coefficients of the two independent variable in question. This, however, is not an issue for this study since the estimated coefficients are statistically significant, and more importantly, "formal federalism' and "size of country" are used here as control variables rather than the main independent variables of interest.

4 Toward a Dynamic Theory of Party Size

In numerous Western industrial democracies, party membership, in both absolute and relative terms, has been shrinking (Katz 1987; Widfeldt 1992). This fact has not been lost on scholars of political parties and democratic politics in general (Crewe 1983; Dalton 1997; Dalton, Flanagan, and Beck 1984; Sainsbury 1985; Katz 1987; Katz and Mair 1995; Selle and Svasand 1991; Pelletier 1995; Messina 1995; Mair 1994; Webb 1995). Nonetheless, despite all the attention in the literature to party decline, there is hardly any literature that examines the effect of party membership decline on party organization and party performance.

The empirical findings based on the cross-sectional model in Chapter Three show that party size has a direct impact on performance and other organizational attributes. More specifically, the findings show that political parties that have large membership size tend to have more complex organization, more centralized distribution of power, and better electoral performance. Since the cross-sectional model is constructed under the assumption of growth in party size, based on the findings in Chapter Three, one may expect to find that declining party size will affect parties' electoral fortunes and lead to shrinking or downsizing of the organizational structures. That is, the relationships observed during period of decline will simply be the reverse of those during period of growth and expansion.

This growth orientation of the literature has led scholars to ignore the fact that organizations may undergo evolutionary phases of birth, growth, stability and then *decline* (Ford 1980a,b). In other words, by simply looking at the cross-sectional model and the relationships of the various attributes, one is left with the impression that the relationships observed during decline will simply be the opposite of those during growth and expansion (Ford 1980a,b). Yet, there is no a priori reason for us to expect that the relationship presented in the cross-sectional model will continue to hold in a dynamic (over time) setting, i.e., in light of declining party membership, for example (Tsouderos 1955; Ford 1980a,b).

Figure 4.1 **Inverse of the Cross-sectional Model**

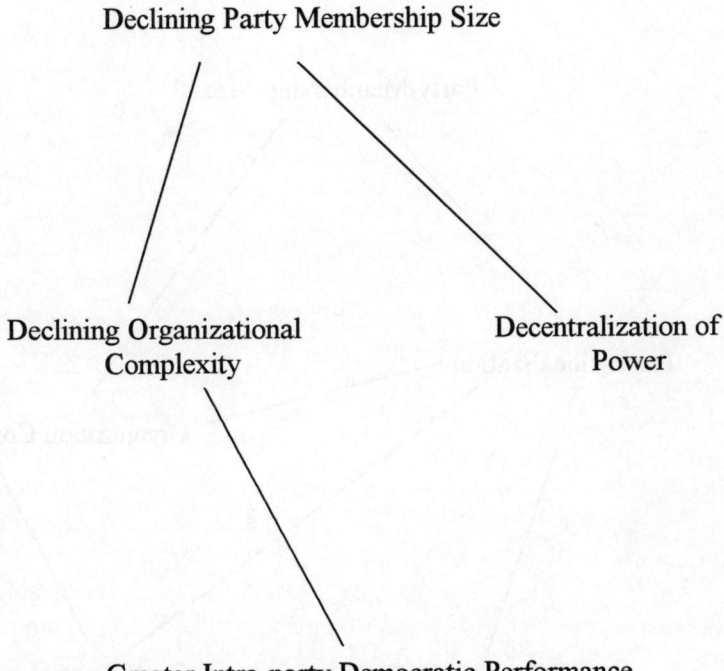

Figure 4.2 **Dynamic Model of Party Membership Size Change**

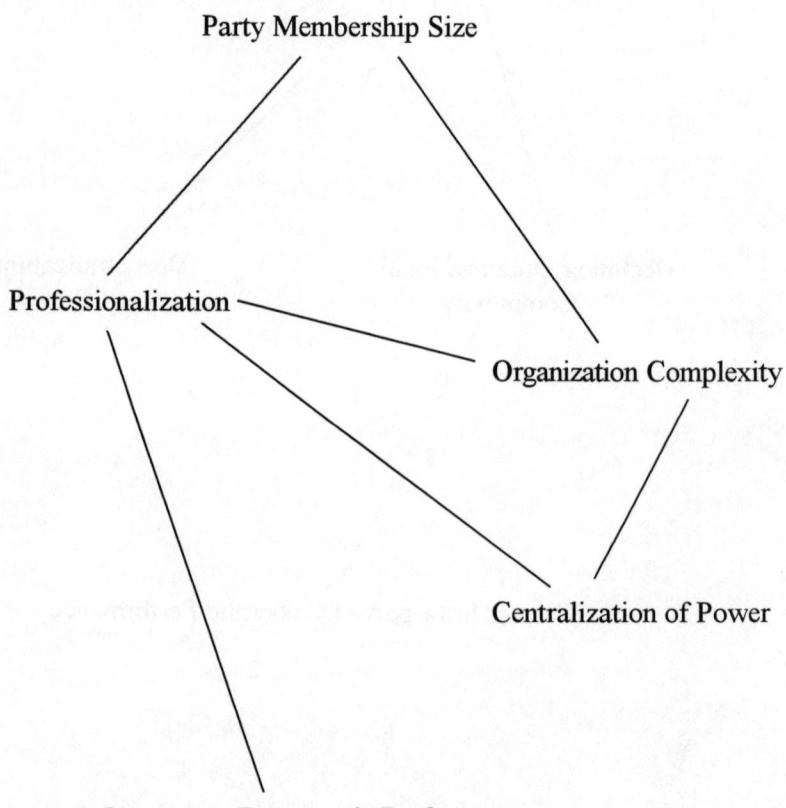

With the advent of advance communications technologies and the employment of these technologies in political parties, doubts have been raised about the relevance of large numbers of members to political parties (Katz 1990; Selle and Svasand 1991). Political parties are believed to have deliberately resorted to these technologies and de-emphasized the importance of large membership thereby resulting in the decline in party membership.[1]

What, then, is the impact of *declining* party size on organizational complexity and on democratic performance? Does party membership size have the same impact over time? Does professionalization replace the need for a complex party organization? Do political parties become more centralized as a result of declining membership? These are some of the questions that need to be addressed in order for us to understand the impact of size on democratic and electoral performance and its impact on political parties as we know them. This study seeks to address the above issue by proposing and testing the dynamic model of the impact of party size. Nonetheless, the goal of this study is not to provide a complete explanation of party performance and organizational forms but rather to determine how much can be explained by the decline in party size.

Party Size and Complexity

Panebianco (1988, 189) suggests that if organizational complexity increases with increase in party size then a decline in party size should lead to a corresponding decline in complexity. Tomasko in his book *Downsizing* notes that firms that have laid off employees have also "flattened" the company pyramid in order to achieve "faster decision-making, quicker awareness of market needs and competitor moves, and lower costs" (1987, 141). To the extent that it is safe to draw parallels between party organization and business organizations, this may lead one to posit that

> Hypothesis 4: As party size declines, organizational complexity will decline.

Contrary to the above argument, Ford (1980b, 626) asserts that changes in the structure of an organization during decline do not reverse those that occur during periods of growth. That is, organizations will not decline in complexity while declining in size. In fact, the null hypothesis that decline in size is not related to decline in complexity has been corroborated by empirical studies of business and voluntary organizations (Tsouderos 1955; Freeman and Hannan 1975; Ford 1980b).

Ford (1980b) posits that the non-responsiveness of organization structure to declining organizational size may be due to so-called coalitional politics within the organization itself. It is argued that as the availability of resources decline, "each member will seek to maintain his or her own position relative to others, the speed with which the organization can adapt is reduced, resulting in hysteresis" (Ford 1980a, 595). That is, as groups seek to insulate their own "turf" from being victims of change, organizational change becomes difficult, if not impossible. Analogously, within political parties "organizational change is more difficult than stasis: implementing such change usually requires an investment of the time and skills of professional organizers, of party leaders' organizational resources, of party money - resources which are often in short supply in any party" (Scarrow 1991, 36).

It is conceivable that the abundance of resources during times of growth allows intra-party politics to be relatively subdued. Decisions pertaining to developing party organizations may generally be non-controversial since "there is enough for everybody" to share. On the other hand, declining party size brings with it (ceteris paribus) other complications such as declining financial resources.[2] Decline in resource availability tends to exacerbate intra-party politics such that control for "turfs" become crucial. These so-called "turf" wars can conceivably affect a party's ability to be responsive to organizational change. It is therefore safe to infer that there may not be a one-to-one correspondence in the decline of party size and decline in organizational complexity. Therefore,

> Hypothesis 4a: As party size declines, the level of organizational complexity remains unchanged.

Professionalization, Organization, and Centralization of Power

"A political organization must be judged by its efficiency in securing victory for the fundamental principles for which the Party stands" (Conservative Party 1949, 28 from Scarrow 1991, 36). If such is the case, poor performance may result in calls for changes in how a political party is delivering its message to the electorate. Party professionalization is one method that may be adopted in order to increase effectiveness. While party professionalization is not clearly defined in the literature, scholars have tended to focus on a few central concepts: employment of experts and consultants, the increasing number of staff and personnel in central party organizations, and the use of communications technologies (see Farrell and Webb 1992; Katz and Mair 1995).[3] In this study, my working definition is based on these concepts as well. Table 4.1 shows the growth of staff members at the party central office and parliamentary delegations for selected political parties in Denmark, Germany, and the United Kingdom.

Table 4.1   Number of Party Staff

	1969	1989
Denmark		
KF	9	43
V	16	37
RV	6	9
SD	35	78
Germany		
CDU	315	1505
FDP	35	278
SPD	166	978
United Kingdom		
Conservative	97	100
Labour	50	81

Source: Katz and Mair 1992.

It is important to note, however, that professionalization may be a deliberate action by the political party as it weighs the costs and benefits of large membership vis-a-vis new alternatives, rather than a reaction to poor performance alone. As early as 1955, R.T. McKenzie concluded in his study of British political parties that effectiveness of mass media technology may affect membership size and party organization. He states,

> It seems likely that the really effective electioneering of the future will rely increasingly on the newer mass media of radio and above all, of television. Perhaps in retrospect it will be evident that the mass party saw its heyday during the period when the extension of franchise had created a mass electorate, but there was as yet no effective means of reaching the voters in their own homes (McKenzie 1955, 591).

In a similar note, Katz and Mair (1995) argue that the professionalization of political parties has led to a decline in the need for large membership since roles traditionally played by members are increasingly replaced by the use of modern technologies. These "new technologies enable a small professional organization to efficiently accomplish formerly labor-intensive campaign and fundraising tasks" (Scarrow 1991, 3). Nonetheless, in her extensive study of membership recruitment by the CDU, SPD, British Conservatives, and the British Labour parties, Scarrow (1991, 55-61) presents convincing evidence that political parties have become more professionalized not because parties wanted to replace members but as a stop-gap measure adopted as a reaction to declining membership. Whether professionalization is a deliberate action of party elites or not, it is important for us to investigate the likely impact of party professionalization on power distribution and intra-party participation.

In the 1960s significant developments within political parties led to predictions by scholars that changes in party organization and membership were in the offing. Samuel Beer, in his study of British politics, suggested that professionalization of the party may increase the trend toward moving more power to the center of the party. He argues that,

> One of the more portentous developments of the sixties may have a bearing on these changes. This is the further professionalization of major party functions, especially the making of party policy and the influencing of voters. For in political parties as in government itself, such developments

raise the possibility of substantial technocratic shifts in the structure of power (1969, 418).

He further argues that,

> This major step (professionalization) in political rationalization may also affect the future character of the mass party. Broadly, the effect of the new technology is to enable central units to by-pass intermediary levels and directly to assess and influence voters' opinions. This could mean a shift of important functions, and therefore power, from local to the central offices...If the new technology continues to shift functions to the central agencies, the local parties, and especially the local activists, will decline in importance. Conceivably, in time, a new kind of technocratic cadre party could take the place of the familiar mass party of Collectivist politics (1969, 420).

Indeed, in a study of Norwegian political parties, Selle and Svasand (1991) conclude that the use of mass media and electronic technology have increasingly made the intermediate units in the party less relevant. Scarrow suggests that "if party leaders came to believe that they can get elected without the help of a large membership organization, then they may well be less likely to listen to the demands of party members, or to make concessions in order to retain members: thus, this decreased dependence would strengthen the iron law of oligarchy within parties" (1991, 5). If so, then increasing professionalization of parties may not only lead to the decline in the need for large membership but may also lead to increasing centralization of power within the party. Under the growth orientation of the cross-sectional model, one expects that with the decline in organizational complexity, centralization of power may decline too. In the dynamic model, however, because of the decline in party size and the need to maintain performance, party professionalization plays a key role in mitigating the negative effects of declining organizational complexity on the centralization of power. In other words,

> Hypothesis 5:   The more the party professionalizes, the greater the centralization of power.

Party Size, Complexity, and Intra-party Democratic Performance

One critical concern of Michels is the problem of participation within the political party as it becomes more hierarchical and complex. More specifically, "growth is thought to correspond to increase in the division of labor, and the bureaucratization and centralization of authority. And these transformations are thought to lead to the decline in participation" (Panebianco 1988, 187). Panebianco argues therefore that "changes in size [should] lead to inverse changes in level of participation" (1988, 187). Olson (1965), in the *Logic of Collective Action*, suggests that a small group tends to have more participatory members as the group is able to distribute a more meaningful level of selective incentives.

While these arguments may be valid in a cross-sectional sense, it may be more complicated in a dynamic setting. The level of participation may be affected by organizational complexity. It is logical to posit that increasing levels of organizational complexity may not be conducive to participation of members. While organizational complexity may decline as a result of decrease in size (hypothesis 4), increasing party professionalization may impede the level of democratic performance (or intra-party democracy). Due to these factors, the impact of party size decline on participation is mitigated. That is,

Hypothesis 6: The greater the level of party professionalization, the lower the level of democratic performance.[4]

Party Ideology and Party Organization

In this section, I will briefly discuss the impact of party ideology on party organization which I am employing as a control variable. In his book *Political Parties*, Maurice Duverger suggests that a party's ideology has an influence on how a party organizes and distributes power. Duverger (1963, 21- 39) states that,

> The middle class represented by these parties of the Right does not like the organization and collective action which accompany branches and cells...It is therefore natural that it should always find its political expression within the framework of the caucus...Branches were a Socialist invention: cells are a Communist invention...Just as the cell is a Communist invention, so the militia is a Fascist creation...It is a curious fact [however] that parties based principally on the militia are also very interested in cells and try to give them considerable importance in their organization.

Based on the above one can infer that party ideology is related to the degree of intensiveness of party organization. Though this is only one dimension of party organizational complexity, Duverger also alludes to the impact of party ideology on other dimensions of organizational complexity. He argues that one can distinguish the strength of how party structures are linked together by a party's ideology. He states,

> Socialist parties everywhere are more strongly articulated than Conservative parties, whatever the electoral system...In the nineteenth century parties were based upon...weak articulation; today most Conservative, Moderate, and "Liberal" parties in Europe still display these two essential characteristics (Duverger 1963, 45-46).

Indeed, Janda and King (1985) has found empirical support that party ideology is a statistically significant predictor of the degree of organizational complexity. More specifically, leftist parties tend to have greater organizational complexity than non-leftist parties.

Beyond affecting the degree of complexity of party organization, party ideology is also said to affect the distribution of power in a political party. Duverger suggests that leftist parties tend to be more centralized than non-leftist parties, he states

> Labour parties are less centralized than Communist parties; parties created by capitalist groups are less centralized than Labour parties, and so on (1963, xxxiv).

Furthermore, Duverger (1963, 135) also argues that party ideology can affect the level of intra-party democratic performance. In particular, rightist parties according to Duverger seem to provide for lesser intra-party democracy than leftist parties. For example, Duverger (1963, 135) contends that in fascist parties the "*fuhrer princip* replaces election as the ground of legitimacy" inferring that rightist parties tend to provide lower levels of intra-party democracy.

Based on the above discussion, we should expect that party ideology will exert significant influence on how parties organize. More specifically, our theoretical expectation is that leftist parties will be more organizationally complex, more centralized, and more democratic internally.

Summary

We began this chapter by posing the question: What is the impact of party decline on how parties organize? In the dynamic model I have posited that the decline of party size in Western industrial democracies is bound to have an impact on party structures, unless parties actively mitigate its impact. One way to soften the impact on party structures and organization is for parties to professionalize. While professionalization is not an end-all, be-all, professionalization of political parties has been seen by party elites and scholars alike as a way of making the party adapt to a rapidly changing environment.

In light of the findings of Chapter Three regarding the significance of party size and its impact on other organizational attributes and performance, it would be interesting to see whether the relationships continue to hold in a dynamic setting. In the next chapter, I will empirically test the dynamic model using the still in-progress National Science Foundation supported Party Change project directed by Robert Harmel and Kenneth Janda.

Notes

1. Scarrow (1994) provides an alternative perspective on whether parties are de-emphasizing membership recruitment or not.

2. There are several types of state subsidy to political parties. In Germany, for example, financial support to political parties is tied to the percent of votes garnered in Federal and Land elections. In other countries, financial support is tied to the number of party members.

3. Panebianco defines professionalization as involving the increasing number of experts employed in the party organization. He distinguishes this from "bureaucratization" as growth in political professionals that simply manages the party organization. It is, however, safe to infer from his definitions of administrators and experts that both groups are considered professionals. In my usage of the term professionalization, it encompasses an increase in the employment of administrators, managers, and technologies.

4. The level of democratic performance does not pertain to how active members are (i.e., the quantity) but the quality of the participation. More specifically, democratic performance relates to the role of individual party members in party decision-making.

5   Empirical Tests and Analysis of the Dynamic Model

In Chapter Four I formulated the hypotheses regarding the impact of the decline in party size on party organization and performance. Selle and Svasand argue that the "issue of party decline is...not only a matter of establishing time-series data for appropriate indicators but also of relating such indicators to organizational changes in parties and to contextual factors that may modify their impact" (1991, 468). This is what the model as presented in Chapter Four seeks to explain. In the following sections of this chapter, I will describe the source and nature of the data to be used for the empirical test of the dynamic model. Subsequent to this discussion, I will present and analyze the results of the tests.

Data and Measurement

Ideally, the dynamic model would be subjected to rigorous empirical tests using both cross-national and longitudinal data from all Western industrial democracies. Unfortunately, such an extensive data set is not currently available. A smaller data set collected by Robert Harmel and Kenneth Janda for their Party Change Project provides the only cross-national and longitudinal data on political parties that is currently available. The NSF-supported Party Change Project collected party-level data on 18 political parties from Denmark, Germany, the United Kingdom, and the United States from 1950-1990. For the empirical test of the dynamic model, four political parties from Denmark, three political parties from Germany and the two major parties from the United Kingdom will be included in the sample.[1]

Although the small number of political parties may detract from the generalizability of the findings of this chapter, it does not render the findings useless. The nine political parties currently in the sample operate in relatively different environments, e.g., area size of country, population, electoral system. The electoral system, for example, varies between the three countries in the sample. Denmark has party-list voting with proportional representation system while the United Kingdom has a single-member, plurality system. As shown in the empirical findings of Chapter Three, the differences in the electoral systems alone have vastly different impacts on party performance and organizational attributes (see Harmel and Janda 1982). Furthermore, the longitudinal data collected for the Party Change Project and the Party Organizations Project for the nine political parties of Denmark, Germany and the United Kingdom are sufficient to adequately model and test the "causal process captured in the longitudinal data" (Stimson 1985, 917).

The data for the party level variables - party membership, organizational complexity, centralization of power, party professionalization, and intra-party democratic performance - that are used in the empirical analysis come mainly from two sources: Katz and Mair's Party Organizations Project and Harmel and Janda's Party Change Project. More specifically, data for the main independent variable "party membership size" and other key variables - intra-party democratic performance and party professionalization - were operationalized and measured using data obtained from the Katz and Mair project. Data for the variable "organizational complexity" were operationalized and measured using data obtained from the Harmel and Janda project.[2] The time frame for the data analysis is from 1960 to 1990.[3]

Because the operationalization and measurement of the variables "party membership size," and "organizational complexity" have been extensively discussed in Chapter Three, those discussions will not be repeated here.[4] It is important to mention, however, that the main independent variable - party membership size - will be operationalized as the annual number of direct individual members of a party from 1960 to 1990 as reported in the Katz and Mair Party Organizations data set.[5] In the following sub-sections, I will discuss extensively the operationalization and the source of new variables (e.g. party professionalization and party ideology) introduced in Chapter Four and re-introduce other variables - centralization of power and intra-party democratic performance - that are operationalized slightly differently from Chapter Three.

Party Professionalization

There are several data on party professionalization that are currently available. Unfortunately, most of them do not have time-series data long enough for this study. Often times, surveys collected on party professionalization provide a cross-sectional glimpse of how much a party has professionalized (Farrell and Webb 1992) but not the development of party professionalization which this study requires.

The Party Change Project has a variable on "party professionalization" that was collected by sending survey questionnaires to the respective party secretaries of the party head offices in 1993. The survey taps into the multi-dimensionality of "party professionalization" by collecting information on various items such as: party employees, subcontracting to outside firms, techniques, computerization, administration, and consultants. Respondents were asked to identify when the party hired its first campaign consultants or bought its first computer. While the survey respondents were able to identify when a particular development occurred the responses provided in the survey are not necessarily longitudinal.[6]

For this particular study, I chose to you use a simpler measure of party professionalization. I operationalized party professionalization by using the number of staff members in the party central office and the parliamentary delegation. Though using the number of staff members as a proxy for "party professionalization" does not capture the multidimensional nature of the concept, the number of staff members a party has can provide a good indication of the level of professionalization a particular political party has achieved. The figures for staff members used here are taken from Katz and Mair's Party Organization project data set.

Centralization of Power

The operationalization of distribution of power is slightly different from the one used in Chapter Three. While in Chapter Three I tapped into the horizontal and vertical dimension of distribution of power in party organizations, in this particular chapter I will only look into the horizontal dimension to which much more reliable and readily available data currently exist. I operationalize the concept of distribution of power by adopting the concept developed in Janda's "leadership concentration" variable that was originally developed for the International Comparative Political Parties (ICPP) project. Leadership concentration basically refers "to the number of individuals who constitute the top party hierarchy and who are regarded as key decision makers within the party" (Janda 1980, 116). Janda developed a coding scheme that provides scores for leadership concentration which ranges from 0 to 6 on the following coding scheme shown in Appendix II.

Instead of using Janda's ordinal coding scheme which may limit the variation in the variable, I chose to use an interval and continuous measure of leadership concentration. The Party Organization Project data provides for the size of membership of a political parties' national executive. The size of a party's national executive provides for a good indication of the number of people involved in key decision-making within a political party. Though the "real" decision-making authority may rest in the hands of a smaller group, the membership composition and the size of the party's national executive is a good proxy for measuring whether leadership is concentrated or not. Presumably, the larger the size of the national executive the less concentrated is the leadership of the party.

Intra-party Democratic Performance

In this chapter, intra-party democratic performance is defined as the role of individuals in party affairs and decision making. It is important to note that the variable as used here is slightly different from the operationalization in Chapter Three.[7] In Michel's writing about the role of individuals, he was most concerned with what impact the individuals have on the governance and administration of the party organization. From Michels' writing one may logically infer that in modern political parties two aspects of a party's governance may be open to individual party members' participation - candidate selection and control over party rules.[8]

Candidate selection generally involves the nominating of leaders for elected positions in the national legislature. In fact, in the sample of countries used in this analysis, there is substantial variance in the degree of involvement that is allowed by parties in the process of nomination. For some political parties, individual party members are not given any specified role in the selection of official party candidates, while other parties do not have explicit control of the candidate selection process as in the use of primaries in the United States. Another aspect of intra-party democracy is the role of individual party members in formulating and controlling party rules. Control over party rules involves the role of each organization and/or individual party member in proposing amendments or adoption of rules that regulate party behavior. As in candidate selection, some parties do not provide any role for individual members while others allow parties to propose and vote for amendments to party rules.

Table 5.1   Coding   Scheme   for   Intra-party   Democratic Performance

Control over Candidate Selection
0   No role is specified for individual party members.
1   Party allows individual party members to nominate candidates but party members do not vote for the candidates.
2   Party allows individual party members to vote (or ratify) for nominees or a list of nominees drawn up by some upper level party committee. (Note: this score is given if the party can only vote and not nominate any candidates).
3   Party allows individual party members to propose nominees via local branches and vote for nominees to be official party candidates.
4   Party does not have explicit control over the candidate selection process, e.g. primary election.

Control over Party Rules
0   No role is specified for individual party members.
1   Party allows individual members to propose changes to party rules but upper level party committee is given the final authority to accept or reject proposals.
2   Party allows individual members to vote for proposals that are presented by an upper level party committee.
3   Party allows individual members to submit proposals to change party rules via local branches and members are allowed to vote on the proposals.
4   Party allows individual members to submit proposals directly to the national conference (without approval from any intermediary committee) and members are allowed to vote on the proposals.

For the purposes of this study, I have developed a coding scheme to transform the "raw" data from the Party Organizations data set into standardized codes.[9]   The two indicators of "intra-party democratic performance" include the role of individual party members in candidate selection and the control over party rules.   The indicator "candidate selection" is scored from zero to four, where the higher the score the greater the role of the individual party member in selecting official party candidates in elections. The indicator "control over party rules" is scored from zero to four, where a higher score also means that the individual party member has greater control over party rules (see Table 5.1).

Research Design and Empirical Tests

In Chapter Three, I pointed out that several of the variables used in the analysis are variables that are composites of multiple indicators. Since there are no theoretical justifications to weigh the multiple indicators unequally in computing an index, I weighed them equally by standardizing the scores for each indicator using the z-scoring process. Z-scoring was used to standardize the indicators combined in indices of "organizational complexity."

For the variable "intra-party democratic performance," a standardized index was derived by summing up the two scores for the two indicators - candidate selection and control over party rules. The higher the democratic performance scores, the greater the role specified for individual party members.

For party professionalization, I operationalized this as a simple count of the number of staff members of a party's central office as reported in the Party Organization project data set. In the case of party ideology, a dummy variable is used to identify leftist parties from non-leftist parties. Leftist parties are coded 1, non-leftist parties are coded 0.

Table 5.2   Summary Statistics

Variables	Mean	S. D.	Min.	Max.
Membership Size (log)	12.2	1.4	9.2	14.8
Org. Complexity	-0.4	3.1	-5.8	6.9
Centralization	32.8	19.2	1.0	75.0
Professionalization	158.0	281.5	5.0	1521
Party Ideology	0.33	0.47	0.0	1.0
Intraparty Democracy	0.41	0.27	0.0	0.8

Pooled cross-sectional time-series was used for the empirical test. The summary statistics for the relevant variables are shown in Table 5.2. In the following section I present the results of the empirical tests.

Analysis

Organizational Complexity

Do changes in party membership size affect the complexity of party organization over time? Table 5.3 shows the results of the empirical test. As the results of empirical test show, party membership size is a statistically significant predictor of organizational complexity. That even with the changes in the size of party membership over time in the nine political parties included in the sample, larger membership size is related to more complex party organization.

Table 5.3 also shows that party professionalization has an impact on organizational complexity. More specifically, the greater the level of party professionalization the less complex the party organization. Over the past thirty years, political parties have increasingly become more professionalized in all facets of their operations. Professionalization, it is believed, allows political parties to continue functioning effectively in the electoral arena. Furthermore, it has been argued that by being "professionalized" political parties displace the necessity of having complex organizations since party activities and operations can be centralized in the party head office. As Scarrow points out succinctly "the size of a party's membership may constrain the ways in which it can try to win electoral support. For instance, if a party has a very low *average* membership per constituency, it may either be forced to look outside its own membership for local campaign help, or else try to rely almost entirely on professional, probably centralized, campaigning" (1991, 89).

The evidence provides some credence to the existing arguments that party professionalization displaces the need for complex party organizations in the face of declining levels of party membership. However, it is important to note that because political parties have not attached lesser value to recruitment of prospective party members, party professionalization has been adopted to complement existing organizational structure rather than to totally replace it (Scarrow 1996). There are numerous examples of political parties organizing massive recruitment drives and initiating various programs (e.g., party magazines, newsletters, maintaining a computerized list of membership) in order to increase or maintain current levels of membership or simply to maintain certain levels of communication with their members (Scarrow 1996). All these point to the fact that rather than completely replacing complex organizations, party professionalization can be used to launch such massive recruitment campaigns and electoral campaigns and in turn aid in the maintenance of organizational stability. One official of the British Conservative Party was quoted as saying that despite all the improvements in communications technology "the only really effective way of getting in touch with the electorate, and continuing to stay in touch with them, is by having an active organisation in each town, village and ward in EVERY constituency in the country" (Scarrow 1991, 62).

Table 5.3   Determinants of Organization Complexity

	Estimated Coefficients
Party membership size (log)	1.19***
	(0.13)
Professionalization	-0.07***
	(0.01)
Prof * Members	0.005***
	(0.008)
Left	0.63***
	(0.23)
Electoral system	-3.16***
	(0.28)
Area (log)	3.64
	(3.78)
Population (log)	1.77
	(2.54)
Constant	-5.73
	(11.94)
R-squared	0.88

Note: ***p<0.01;**p<0.05;*p<0.10

Party professionalization, in fact, can be seen as a remedial measure undertaken by political parties to enhance the quality of the party organization. As Selle and Svasand argue

> it could be that the relationship between interest politics and membership has changed or at least become more complex. The cost of exit can be looked at as decreasing because of a weakening of political loyalty. Such a situation would make the parties even more vulnerable, increasing the importance of the quality of the party organization for electoral success (1991, 464).

Consistent with Duverger's proposition, party ideology is found to be statistically significant determinant of party organizational complexity. The results of the empirical test in Table 5.3 show that leftist parties tend to be more organizationally complex vis-a-vis the parties of the right. Take the Danish Social Democrats as a case in point. Of the four Danish parties included in this study, the Danish Social Democrats are the most organizationally complex. In fact, while the Danish Social Democrats experienced some downsizing of their organization in the thirty year period from 1960 to 1990, the party has remained relatively complex.

Cross-national comparisons also show the effect of the electoral system on organizational complexity. The effect of the electoral system is statistically significant at the 0.01 level. We can infer from the results that political parties that operate in more proportional representation systems tend to have more complex party organizations. The empirical data supports this claim when one compares the British and the Danish parties. Denmark has a proportional representation system that has a very low threshold, while the United Kingdom uses the single-member plurality system. Between these two countries, Danish political parties (on average) are more organizationally complex than the two British parties included in this study.

Centralization of Power

What is the impact of changing party membership on centralization of power? Reading Michels' work on the SPD, it may be reasonable to infer that an increase in party size tends to lead to increasing centralization of power. The empirical findings in Chapter Three support the hypothesis that as party size increases centralization of power tends to increase up to a certain point. Relating back to the hypotheses presented in Chapter Four, hypothesis 5 leads us to expect that increasing level of professionalization will lead to more centralization of power at the national level. Table 5.4 reports the results of the statistical analysis.

Party membership size continues to exert significant influence on the centralization of power in a political party. As the empirical results show and consistent with the findings in Chapter Three, larger party membership size tends to be associated with greater level of centralization of power.

Table 5.4   Determinants of Centralization of Power

	Estimated Coefficients
Party membership size (log)	9.03***
	(0.69)
Professionalization	-0.07**
	(0.04)
Prof * Members	0.004*
	(0.003)
Left	-16.34***
	(1.21)
Electoral system	-0.07
	(1.39)
Area (log)	-186.23***
	(21.26)
Population (log)	136.09***
	(14.16)
Constant	-710.68***
	(65.19)
R-squared	0.81

Note: ***$p<0.01$;**$p<0.05$;*$p<0.10$

Contrary to the expectation of hypothesis 5, however, the empirical results show that greater the level of party professionalization leads to less centralization of power. However, this is tempered by the interaction between professionalization and party membership size. Despite the fact that increasing levels of party professionalization may lead to greater centralization of power, the size of party membership puts certain limits to the degree of decentralization of power in a party.

As with Duverger's assertion that leftist parties tend to be less centralized, the results of the empirical test provide support for that assertion. Indeed, the impact of party ideology on centralization of power is strongly significant at the 0.01 level.

Turning to electoral system, it is interesting to note here that Duverger (1963, 45) suggested that proportional representation systems tend to promote stronger party organization while single-member plurality systems tend to weaken party organization. Besides suggesting that electoral systems affect the level of organizational complexity, it is also possible to infer from Duverger's argument that proportional representation systems, rather than single-member plurality system, would tend to be associated with parties that have higher levels of centralization of power. The available evidence does not seem to support this expectation.

Intra-party Democratic Performance

Do changes in party membership size lead to increasing levels of intra-party democratic performance as reversing Michels' thesis would lead one to believe? Does increasing level of party professionalization affect the level of intra-party democratic performance? Hypothesis 6 leads us to expect that a decline in party membership size coupled with increasing levels of professionalization should lead to lower levels of democratic performance. Table 5.5 shows the results of the statistical analysis.

The evidence suggests that professionalization is significantly related to intra-party democratic performance. That is, higher level of party professionalization is associated with lower level of intra-party democratic performance. This finding is in line with the expectation stated in hypothesis 6. It is important to note that declining party size is not related to intra-party democratic performance. Contrary to expectations, leftist parties tend to have lower level of intra-party democratic performance.

Table 5.5   Determinants of Intra-party Democratic Performance

	Estimated Coefficients
Party membership size	0.003
	(0.02)
Professionalization	-0.005***
	(0.001)
Prof * Members	0.0004***
	(0.00008)
Left	-0.23***
	(0.02)
Electoral system	-0.008
	(0.02)
Area (log)	-2.96***
	(0.41)
Population (log)	2.03***
	(0.28)
Constant	-8.36***
	(1.29)
R-squared	0.57

Note: ***$p<0.01$; **$p<0.05$; *$p<0.10$

Interestingly, the interactive effect of party professionalization and party membership size shows that it enhances intra-party democratic performance. In some sense, the interaction of party membership size with increasing professionalization can temper the dampening effect of party professionalization on intra-party democratic performance. As numerous studies have shown, the importance of membership cannot be underestimated even in the face of increasing party professionalization that seems to be undertaken to marginalize the membership itself (Mair 1994; Scarrow 1991, 1996).

Ware suggests that "changes in western economies, and particularly the declining relative importance of manufacturing industry, have produced new social groups that lack the traditional ties to class-based parties" (1987, 220). Furthermore, with the rise in the educational level in these societies, political parties are facing a more elite-challenging membership that increasingly demands more participatory role in party decision-making. As a consequence, political parties may provide more participatory opportunities to make party membership more attractive to this new type of prospective members.

In a similar vein, Mair (1994, 5) notes that

> far from marginalizing their members, a variety of different parties are actually ceding them more decision-making power...the British Labour Party allowed representatives of the membership a direct vote in leadership elections...Party members in Denmark...now have a greater role in candidate selection as well as a voice in the approval of party programmes...In Germany, the SPD is now emphasizing the need for greater Basisdemokratie, including the introduction of binding membership ballots.

He further states that

> it also seems that many parties are attempting to give their members more say rather than less say, and that they are empowering them rather than marginalizing them. Many parties now afford their ordinary members a greater voice in candidate selection than was once the case...more and more parties now seem willing to allow the ordinary members a voice in the selection of party leaders (Mair 1994, 15).

Indeed in various country chapters on Katz and Mair's book, *How Parties Organize*, individual country experts provide strong and rich evidence of the increasing opportunities for participation in political parties in spite of increasing levels of party professionalization.

All these evidences are indeed good news for students of political parties and party change since they signal that political parties as organizations are adaptive and relatively responsive organizations. Nonetheless, one should be cautioned that what is measured as intra-party democratic performance in this particular study reflects the formal rules as provided for by each party to individual party members rather than the actual behavior of party members. Furthermore, these evidences should be tempered by the fact that as Mair puts it "intra-party democratization is often illusory," that is "democratization on paper may...coexist with powerful elite influence in practice" (Mair 1994, 16-17).

Even with these sobering note, though, the formal rules that provides for more participation by individual party members have changed in the thirty year period from 1960 to 1990. The nine political parties, in this study, have provided for more participation by individual members in a formal sense. This increase in the level of intra-party democratic performance comes at the heels of changing levels of party membership (declining membership levels) and also at increasing levels of party professionalization.

Summary

In Chapters One and Three, I posed the question: What is the impact of declining party membership on a party's electoral and democratic performance? This question is the main focus of Chapter Four and the empirical tests in this current chapter. A secondary concern of this chapter is on the impact of changing levels of party membership size on organizational complexity and centralization of power.

In the literature, there are two contrasting answers regarding the impact of party size on party performance and party organization. One perspective is from Robert Michels classic book on political parties. From Michel', one may infer that organizational size is the primary independent variable from which other changes derive. That is, "Michels' theory [can be summarized as] growth in size is considered to be the cause of every change a party undergoes" (Panebianco 1988, 185). In arguing his case, Michels provides evidence on the impact of organizational growth of the German Social Democratic Party on the party organization itself. This perspective on the primacy of party size is contrasted by Panebianco's claim that size does not have any independent impact on party organization and performance at all. By providing anecdotal evidence, Panebianco concludes that "size in and of itself, does not seem responsible for significant variations in political style, participation, [and] complexity" (1988, 190). How do the empirical findings of this study address this debate? Where does it stand with regards to the impact of party size?

From the systematic analysis of available time-series data of nine political parties in Denmark, Germany and the United Kingdom, the empirical findings of this study largely supports Michels' proposition that party membership size does have an impact on how political parties organize and how power is distributed in a political party. That being said, party membership size does not have an independent impact on the level of intra-party democratic performance as is operationalized here.

Nonetheless, it is important to note here that while party membership size is an important determinant of the complexity of party organization and its distribution of power, other factors are also important. Factors such as party ideology, electoral system, and other environmental variables also exert influence on organizational complexity and centralization of power. The empirical analysis done here reinforces existing study of complex organizations by showing that environmental factors remain important predictors of party organizations but it also add to it by showing that internal party structural factors, such as party membership size, are also key ingredients to our understanding of how party organizes.

Reflecting further on the available evidence and findings of this chapter, one is led to more questions about the type of political parties that currently exist in advanced industrial democracies. The findings in this chapter suggest that though political parties are experiencing some decline in its membership ranks in general they continue to persist as organizations. At the same time, political parties continue to dominate the political scene in their respective polities. Are political parties really in decline? Are they dinosaurs that will eventually become extinct in a changing political landscape? We will be remiss not to examine these questions in light of the extensive debate that currently exists on the question of whether political parties as we know it are in decline or not. In the concluding chapter of this book, I will try to address these important questions.

Notes

1. The two American parties were excluded in the analysis because the key independent variable, party membership, is not a relevant concept in the United States. The exclusion of the British Liberal Party and four other Danish political parties, was an artifact of unavailable data on key variables, such as, organizational complexity, centralization of power, and leadership concentration. In Janda's original International Comparative Political Parties (ICPP) project, he included parties that consistently win more than 5 percent of the electoral votes during the period 1950-1962. This effectively excluded the British Liberal Party from the sample since the party has been replaced by the British Labour Party as the second party in the UK. In the case of Denmark, the newer parties do not qualify in the time frame used in the ICPP project. In both the current and the ICPP project, Janda only collected data for the Danish Social Democrats, Danish Liberals, Danish Conservatives, and Danish Radical Liberals (or Social Liberals).

2. The information and data collected for the Party Change Project encompass a wide range of party level variables, these variables include: parliamentary vs. extraparliamentary party relations; dominant factions; leadership; primary goals; professionalization; issues; organizational complexity; centralization of power; coherence.

3. It is important to note here that because the Katz and Mair project collected data from 1960-1990 while the Harmel and Janda project collected data from 1950-1990, the time frame for the data analysis used in this study has to be limited to 1960-1990.

4. Except for professionalization, the variables "organizational complexity" and "centralization of power" are extensions of Janda's ICPP project. The only difference between these two projects with regards to these two variables is that the Party Change project's data is longitudinal (from 1950-1990), while the ICPP project assigned an average score for each half of the 12-year period from 1950-1962.

5. The operationalization for party size used here is slightly different from the one used in Chapter Three. In Chapter Three, party size is operationalized as the average number of direct individual party members from 1960-1962.

6. In their study of party professionalization, Farrell and Webb (1992) attempted to capture the multi-dimensionality of professionalization, although they never provided a conceptual definition of it. In their cross-sectional survey of major West European parties, Farrell and Webb requested these parties to provide information as to whether they hired campaign consultants, use radio and television for political advertisement, has their own party newspaper etc. This effort is commendable and a good first step to tap into and develop this key variable "party professionalization" that the literature mentions but not provide much in the way of definition and data. If there is any shortcoming in the Farrell and Webb (1992) study, it is mainly due to the cross-sectional nature of the survey instrument. As an illustration, Farrell and Webb asked parties to provide information about whether they used a television advertisements, for example, in one particular parliamentary election. Consequently, the information does not provide a historical perspective as to when certain staff, consultants, and/or technology were adopted. Due to the nature of the survey instrument used, the data collected are not appropriate for longitudinal analysis required in this study. The Party Change Project data on party professionalization, to a certain extent, addressed this shortcoming of the Farrell and Webb survey on party professionalization. This is not to say, however, that the survey instrument used by the Party Change Project is necessarily flawless.

7. In Chapter Three, intra-party democratic performance was operationalized as the number of active members in the party.

8. Bille (1994) also used the Katz and Mair data set to study the development of the role of individual party members in political parties. Bill's study, however, did not develop a coding scheme that can be used for quantitative analysis.

9. It is important to note that the "data" in both projects are in different formats. For the Party Change Project, information from secondary sources was "scored" based on a judgmental coding scheme and the scheme was applied consistently for the parties included in the data set. For the Party Organization Project, the data consist of "raw" information from party documents and sources. In order to make the two data sets compatible, coding schemes would have to be devised to translate these "raw" information into specific "scores" that make the data usable for quantitative analysis.

6 Conclusion

What is the impact of declining party size on electoral and democratic performance? This is the main research question that has led to this study. The findings in Chapter Five lead us to conclude that together with factors such as party professionalization, party ideology and environmental variables, party membership size significantly impacts how political parties organize, how it distributes power, and how it provides participatory opportunities for its members.

Having summarized the findings of this study one is left to ponder: What do these findings tell us about whether political parties are in decline or not? Are they dinosaurs that will eventually become extinct in a changing political landscape? This will be the main focus of this concluding chapter. The question of whether political parties are in decline or not can be examined in several ways. First, we can examine the issue of political parties and their relation to civil society. In this perspective, one is concerned with the linkage function that political parties are supposed to perform. Secondly, we can observe the strength of party organizations. That is, whether party organizations continue to be maintained can provide us an indication of whether political parties are declining or not.[1] In the following section I address these questions in an attempt to give an answer to whether political parties are in decline or not.

Whither Political Parties?

The Linkage Factor

What is the state of relation between political parties and civil society? Do political parties continue to function well as a linkage mechanism? As far as the findings of this study are concerned, it is quite evident that political parties are experiencing continued decline in the levels of party membership despite measures undertaken by political parties to counter this trend. There are various explanations as to why political parties continue to be battered by declining membership levels, but probably the most oft cited is that membership decline is a consequence of the development of postindustrial societies. Poguntke explains that the

> processes of social modernization and value change have increasingly undermined the formerly stable relations of mass parties with their electorates and core of loyal supporters or even party members...[therefore] Individuals are more prone to loosen their traditional ties to parties - or less likely to establish them in the first place (1995, 2).

Along the same lines, Katz argues that

> the success of social service programs has been the breakdown of the solidarity of many of the social groups that formed one basis of party cohesion in the past (Katz 1990, 145).

Likewise, Dalton (1997) suggests that there are both macro-level and micro-level changes that have mitigated the roles of political parties and may therefore be factors in explaining the decline in partisanship. Macro-level factors such as the changes in mass media and the erosion of group-based politics have eroded the roles that political parties traditionally play in a democratic polity. Dalton (1997, 5) states that

> the mass media are assuming many of the information functions that political parties once controlled. Instead of learning about an election at a campaign rally or from party canvassers, television and newspapers have become the primary sources of campaign information. Furthermore, the content of the mass media has changed to downplay the importance of political parties and even adopt anti-partisan or anti-elite tone.

At the micro-level, Dalton (1997, 6) argues that increasing educational levels have resulted in a more sophisticated electorate that relies less on parties and party elites for political information. That is, this type of "cognitive mobilization" has led to the electorate being more self-sufficient and more active in non-partisan types of political participation (Dalton 1996). Furthermore, Dalton (1997, 6) claims that value changes as a result of the modernization process in advanced industrial democracies have resulted in political issues that "cut across existing partisan alignments...[and] are not well represented in contemporary party systems."

All the above are very strong and credible explanations of why parties continue to be battered by declining memberships and to a certain extent "marginalized" in the eyes of many members of the electorate. However, to conclude that political parties are failing as linkage mechanisms between civil society and government by citing the decline in party membership levels may be too stringent.[2] In order for us to be able to claim that parties have declined as a result of the declining partisanship, we should be able to show that decline in party membership has seriously affected the ability of political parties to function as a linkage mechanism. What does this linkage mean? As Widfeldt (1999) suggests the use of this particular concept, though often used in political science, is vague and confusing. One good definition of the term linkage is provided by Poguntke (1995, 3) as he states that

> the function of linkage has been the same since the advent of democratic politics. Parties need stable means of communicating with their electorates in order to identify, select and aggregate relevant grievances, communicate them to the higher echelons of politics and strive for policies which take account of these political demands.

It is in this particular form of linkage that party members play an important role. Party members are society's eyes and ears, so to speak. In that sense, political parties are able to garner public opinion and other feedback by having a party membership composition that reflects the electorate.

Likewise, Widfeldt (1999, 8-22) in a thorough discussion of the linkage role of political parties also suggests that political parties provide participatory and representative linkages. A political party is said to perform a participatory linkage by providing opportunities for citizens to participate in internal party affairs. It performs a representative linkage when citizen's interests are accounted for in party decisions and policies. Some scholars have argued that because the levels of party membership are declining, this form of linkage is in decline (Katz 1990).

There is "no doubt, [that] organizational linkage provides [a] kind of linkage, because built-in organizational thresholds and formalized procedures of decision-making serve to select and aggregate demands which are channeled through the organization to party elites" (Poguntke 1995, 3). It can be argued, however, that despite the predominance of linkage through traditional organizational connections, linkage between civil society and political parties can be undertaken by means other than traditional organizational connections. In other words, the same linkage function can also be performed using mechanisms other than having huge membership in the party organization.

The available evidence of declining party size (or membership) coupled with increasing levels of party professionalization suggest that political parties continue to perform their linkage function, albeit in a different form. While in the past, parties may have relied on party activists for feedback on prevailing public opinion, today's political parties have increasingly relied on public opinion survey and modern mass communication technology (such as television and the internet) to perform the same linkage function between political parties and their electorate (Katz 1990; Selle and Svasand 1991). Indeed as "modern campaign techniques [became] more important...parties found themselves increasingly forced to develop new strategies to reach those who remained outside the realm of organizational politics" (Poguntke 1995, 6). This increasing reliance on mass communication technology and public opinion surveys is evidence that political parties are not necessarily neglecting to perform as a link between civil society and state. It is important to note, though, that the form and shape of this linkage function is, to a large extent, changing. As Katz explains

> television has become the dominant source of political information and the dominant channel of communication from elites to the public, with the party meeting, the party canvaser, the party press, all supplanted in importance by the party leader speaking directly to his or her supporters on the small screen. Moreover, state financial support to political parties has allowed the parties...to insulate themselves financially from their members as well. These developments have changed, or threaten to change, the very character of the political party...Party increasingly becomes an organization of leaders rather than of citizens (Katz 1990, 146).

Beyond stating that political parties are not shirking from their linkage role but instead changing the form of the linkage, neither the data nor the empirical findings of this study are able to evaluate the effectiveness of this linkage through these alternative mechanisms. It is at least important to note, however, that in the debate regarding the declining ability of parties to perform their linkage role, scholars have cited the rise in the number of citizen initiatives, single-issue groups, or social movements as a sign that political parties are not performing this function adequately (Dalton 1996; Ware 1987, 1996). As Katz suggests that

> a host of new single-issue and new politics interest groups and alternative

parties have arisen catering to demands for direct participation and competing with the established parties as channels of communication between the public and the state (Katz 1990, 145).

However, Selle and Svasand argue that "ad hoc movements are less of a competitor for parties than it first seemed...[and] that ad hoc movements are more of a supplement to parties than an alternative" (1991, 468). It may be the case that rather than indicating party ineffectiveness in performing its linkage function, the rise in single-issue groups may indicate that political parties are either specializing in their own issue concerns or are still formulating their stands on the new issues brought to the political arena by these alternative groups. Kriesi and Van Praag, in fact, found that in the case of the peace movement in the Netherlands, movement activists "have strong and extensive relations with the traditional political organizations" (1987, 324). Based on this discussion, it is still true, then, that political parties are not necessarily neglecting their linkage role in society but instead changing the appearance and packaging of that linkage.

Party Organizations

What is the state of party organizations over the past three decades? Have party organizations declined?

Available evidence suggests that political parties continue to persist as organizations in spite of shrinking party size. If one simply observes that the levels of party organizational complexity have not declined dramatically, one may conclude from this one indicator that political parties are not in decline.

We should be cautioned, however, not to equate the persistence in the levels of organizational complexity with active and vibrant organizations. Indeed, the counter-argument is that while political parties continue to be complex and hierarchical organizations, the multi-tiered party organizations may not be functioning, i.e., activity levels may have declined tremendously. Selle and Svasand (1991, 465-467) cite evidences from Norwegian political parties that show that the levels of party activity by individual members are quite moderate. Unfortunately, there are no available data that directly taps the activity levels of political party organizations.

That being said, though, it is important to note that in the the previous section I argued that the traditional form of linkage is increasingly being replaced by a new form of linkage that emphasizes the use of technology and other modern techniques rather than party members. It can be argued, then, that because of the change in the form of linkage, traditional indicators of party activity levels may not be appropriate for this new "type" of political party, i.e., a party with fewer members and more professionalized.

Indeed, one of the most dramatic changes in political parties that we have witness over the past three decades is the transformation from a membership-based party organization to a professionalized party organization. In fact, the available evidence supports this view. It is quite plausible, then, that the dramatic transformation away from membership-based parties to professional parties may be a factor explaining the modest membership activity levels found in most party organizations. In general, despite a likely decline in membership activity levels in most political parties, evidences of the persistence of party organization and the increasing levels of party professionalization seem to indicate a more "dynamic" party organization than a first impression will provide.

Concluding Remarks

Are political parties "dinosaurs" of a bygone era? In addressing the issue of whether political parties are in decline or not, I have suggested that we can evaluate the linkage function being performed by political parties and we can examine the state of party organizations. Based on the available evidence and the arguments presented here, it is prudent to conclude that parties are not in decline and continue to perform their role in the political system. Political parties continue to be a link between the citizens and the state, albeit in a different form. Party organizations continue to persist but are more professionalized rather than membership-based. All these evidences point to the fact that rather than being political dinosaurs, political parties have survived and transformed themselves. By transforming themselves political parties continue to play an active role in democratic politics.

Notes

1. A third way of addressing the question of party decline is by examining whether political parties continue to perform the functions we normally associate with them. The four main functions generally singled out in the literature are: education, interest articulation, interest aggregation, and selection and recruitment of leaders (Harmel and Janda 1978). The functions of education, interest articulation, and interest aggregation are related to the issue of linkage. Unfortunately, the organizational focus and findings of this study do not lend themselves to evaluate whether political parties are performing their functions effectively.

2. Katz and Mair (1995) suggest that political parties are increasingly becoming cartel parties instead of the catch-all parties of the past.

Bibliography

Albinsson, Per. 1986. *Skifningar i blatt: Forandringar insm Moderata Samlingspartiets riksorganisation 1960-1986*. Lund, Sweden: Lummunfaktr Forlag.

Bardi, Luciano. 1992. "The Empirical Study of Party Membership Change." Paper presented at the Workshop on "Democracies and the Organization of Political Parties," ECPR Joint Sessions, University of Limerick, Ireland, 30 March - 4 April.

Beer, Samuel. 1969. *British Politics in the Collectivist Age*. New York: Vintage Books.

Bille, Lars. 1992. "Denmark." In Richard S. Katz and Peter Mair (eds.) *Party Organizations*. London: Sage Publications.

Bille, Lars. 1994. "Denmark: The Decline of the Membership Party?" In Richard S. Katz and Peter Mair (eds.) *How Parties Organize: Change and Adaptation in Party Organizations in Western Democracies*. London: Sage Publications.

Blau, Peter M. 1970. "A Formal Theory of Differentiation in Organizations." *American Sociological Review* 35:201-218.

Blau, Peter M. and Richard Schoenherr. 1971. *The Structure of Organizations*. New York: Basic Books.

Blondel, Jean. 1969. *Introduction to Comparative Government*. New York: Praeger Publishers.

Blondel, Jean. 1978. *Political Parties: A Genuine Case for Discontent?* London: Wildwood House.

Child, John and Roger Mansfield. 1972. "Technology, Size, and Organization Structure." *Sociology* 6:369-393.

Cotter, Cornelius P., James L. Gibson, John F. Bibby, and Robert J. Huckshorn. 1989. *Party Orgnization in American Politics*. New York: Praeger.

Crewe, Ivor. 1983. "The Electorate: Partisan Dealignment Ten Years On." *West European Politics* 6:183-213.

Crotty, William J. 1971. "Party Effort and Its Impact on the Vote." *American Political Science Review* 65: 439-450.

Dalton, Russell J. 1996[1988]. *Citizen Politics in Western Democracies: Public Opinion and Political Parties in the United States, Great Britain, West Germany, and France,* Second Edition. Chatham, New Jersey: Chatham House.

Dalton, Russell J. 1997. "Parties without Partisans: The Decline of Party Identification Among Democratic Publics." Paper presented at the Workshop on "Change in the Relationship of Parties and Democracy," Texas A&M University, College Station, Texas.

Dalton, Russell J, Scott C. Flanagan, and Paul Allen Beck (eds.). 1984. *Electoral Change in Advanced Industrial Democracies: Realignment or Dealignment?* Princeton: Princeton University Press.

Day, Alan J. and Henry W. Degenhart (eds.). 1984. *Political Parties of the World*. Detroit: Gale.

Duverger, Maurice. 1967 [1963]. *Political Parties: Their Organization and Activity in the Modern State*. New York: John Wiley and Sons.

Epstein, Leon. 1967. *Political Parties in Western Democracies*. New York: Praeger.

Farrell, David and Paul Webb. 1992. "The Professionalization of Party Organizations." Paper presented to the Workshop on "Democracies and the Organization of Political Parties," ECPR Joint Sessions, University of Limerick, Ireland, 30 March - 4 April.

Ford, Jeffrey D. 1980a. "The Occurrence of Structural Hysteresis in Declining Organizations." *Academy of Management Review* 5:589-598.

Ford, Jeffrey D. 1980b. "The Administrative Component in Growing and Declining Organizations: A Longitudinal Analysis." *Academy of Management Journal* 23:415-630.

Franklin, Mark, Tom Mackie, and Henry Valen (eds.). 1992. *Electoral Change: Responses to Evolving Social and Attitudinal Structures in Western Countries*. Cambridge: Cambridge University Press.

Freeman, John H. and Michael T. Hannan. 1975. "Growth and Decline Processes in Organizations." *American Sociological Review* 40:215-228.

Frendreis, John P., James L. Gibson, and Laura L. Vertz. 1990. "The Electoral Relevance of Local Party Organizations." *American Political Science Review* 84:225-235.

Gerlich, Peter. 1987. "Consociationalism to Competition: The Austrian Party System Since 1945." In Hans Daalder (ed.) *Party Systems in Denmark, Austria, Switzerland, The Netherlands, and Belgium*. London: Pinter.

Gibson, James L., Cornelius P. Cotter, John F. Bibby, and Robert J. Huckshorn. 1983. "Assessing Party Organizational Strength." *American Journal of Political Science* 27:193-222.

Gibson, James L., Cornelius P. Cotter, John F. Bibby, and Robert J. Huckshorn. 1985. "Whither the Local Parties?: A Cross-Sectional and Longitudinal Analysis of the Strength of Party Organizations." *American Journal of Political Science* 29:139-160.

Greene, William H. 1993. *Econometric Analysis*, Second Edition. New York: Macmillan.

Gujarati, Damodar N. 1988. *Basic Econometrics*, Second Edition. New

York: McGraw-Hill.

Hall, Richard H. 1977. *Organizations: Structure and Process*. Englewood Cliffs, New Jersey: Prentice-Hall.

Hall, Richard H., J. Eugene Haas, and Norman Johnson. 1967. "An Examination of Blau-Scott and Etzioni Typologies." *Administrative Science Quarterly* 12:118-139.

Harmel, Robert. 1989. "The Iron Law of Oligarchy Revisited." In Bryan D. Jones (ed.) *Leadership and Politics: New Perspectives in Political Science*. Lawrence, Kansas: University Press of Kansas.

Harmel, Robert and Kenneth Janda. 1978. *Comparing Political Parties*. Washington, D.C.: The American Political Science Association.

Harmel, Robert and Kenneth Janda. 1982. *Parties and Their Environments*. New York: Longman.

Harmel, Robert and Kenneth Janda. 1994. "An Integrated Theory of Party Goals and Party Change." *Journal of Theoretical Politics* 6:259-287.

Harmel, Robert, Uk Heo, Alexander Tan, and Kenneth Janda. 1995. "Performance, Leadership, Factions, and Party Change: An Empirical Analysis." *West European Politics* 18: 1-33.

Heidar, Knut. 1992. "The Polymorphic Nature of Party Membership: The Unfortunate Habit of Comparing Apples with Oranges in Party Research." Paper presented at the Workshop on "Democracies and the Organization of Political Parties," ECPR Joint Sessions, University of Limerick, Ireland, 30 March - 4 April.

Hermet, G., J. Hottinger, and D. L. Seiler. 1998. *Les Partis Politiques en Europe de l'Ouest*. Paris: Economica.

Herrnson, Paul. 1986. "Do Parties Make a Difference? The Role of Party Organization in Congressional Elections." *Journal of Politics* 48:589-615.

Hill, Kim Quaile and Jan E. Leighley. 1993. "Party Ideology, Organization, and Competitiveness as Mobilizing Forces in Gubernatorial Elections." *American Journal of Political Science* 37:1158-1178.

Huckfeldt, Robert and John Sprague. 1992. "Political Parties and Electoral Mobilization: Political Structure, Social Structure, and Party Canvass." *American Political Science Review* 86:70-86.

Jacques, Martin. 1995. "End of Politics." In Christian Soe (ed.) *Comparative Politics 95/96*. Guilford, Connecticut: Dushkin.

Janda, Kenneth. 1979. "Variations in Party Organization Across Nations and Differences in Party Performance." Paper presented at the 1979 Annual Meeting of the American Political Science Association, The Washington Hilton Hotel, August 31-September 3.

Janda, Kenneth. 1980. *Political Parties: A Cross-national Survey*. New York: Free Press.

Janda, Kenneth. 1983. "Cross-National Measures of Party Organizations and Organizational Theory." *European Journal of Political Research* 11:319-332.

Janda, Kenneth and Desmond King. 1985. "Formalizing and Testing Duverger's Theories." *Comparative Political Studies* 18:139-169.

Janda, Kenneth, Robert Harmel, Christine Edens, and Patricia Goff. 1995. "Changes in Party Identity: Evidence from Party Manifestos." *Party Politics* 1:171-196.

Katz, Daniel and Samuel J. Eldersveld. 1961. "The Impact of Local Party Activity upon the Electorate.' *Public Opinion Quarterly* 25: 1-24.

Katz, Richard S. (ed.). 1987. *Party Governments: European and American Experiences*. Berlin/New York: de Gruyter.

Katz, Richard S. 1990. "Party as Linkage: A Vestigial Function?" *European*

Journal of Political Research 18:143-161.

Katz, Richard S. and Robin Kolodny. 1994. "Party Organizations as an Empty Vessel: Parties in American Politics." In Richard S. Katz and Peter Mair (eds.) *How Parties Organize: Change and Adaptation in Party Organizations in Western Democracies*. London: Sage Publications.

Katz, Richard S. and Peter Mair. 1992. *Party Organization: A Data Handbook*. London: Sage Publications.

Katz, Richard S. and Peter Mair. 1995. "Changing Models of Party Organization: The Emergence of the Cartel Party." *Party Politics* 1: 5-28.

Katz, Richard S. and Peter Mair (eds.). 1994. *How Parties Organize: Change and Adaptation in Party Organizations in Western Democracies*. London: Sage Publications.

Kennedy, Peter. 1992. *A Guide to Econometrics*, Third Edition. Cambridge, Massachusetts: MIT Press.

Key, V.O., Jr. 1964. *Politics, Parties and Pressure Groups*, Fifth Edition. New York: Crowell.

Kimberly, John R. 1976. "Organizational Size and the Structuralist Perspective: A Review, Critique, and Proposal." *Administrative Science Quarterly* 21:571-597.

Kirchheimer, Otto. 1966. "The Transformation of the Western European Party Systems." In Joseph LaPalombara and Myron Weiner (eds.) *Political Parties and Political Development*. Princeton: Princeton University Press.

Koelble, Thomas. 1991. *The Left Unravelled: Social Democracy and the New Left Challenge in Britain and West Germany*. Durham: Duke University Press.

Koole, Ruud. 1996. "Cadre, Catch-all or Cartel? A Comment on the Notion of the Cartel Party." *Party Politics* 2: 507-525.

Kriesi, Hanspeter. and P. Van Praag, Jr. 1987. "Old and New Politics: The Dutch Peace Movement and the Traditional Political Organizations." *European Journal of Political Research* 15:319-346.

Lawrence, Paul R. and Jay W. Lorsch. 1967. *Organization and Environment: Managing Differentiation and Integration.* Homewood, Illinois: Richard D. Irwin, Inc.

Lawson, Kay (ed.). 1990. *Political Parties and Linkage: A Comparative Perspective.* New Haven: Yale University Press.

Lipset, Seymour Martin. 1962. "Introduction." In Robert Michels, *Political Parties: A Sociological Study of the Oligarchical Tendencies of Modern Democracy.* New York: Free Press.

Lipset, Seymour Martin. 1963. *Political Man: Social Bases of Politics.* New York: Anchor.

Lipset, Seymour Martin and Stein Rokkan. 1967. *Party Systems and Voter Alignments.* New York: Free Press.

Mair, Peter. 1994. "Party Organizations: From Civil Society to the State." In Richard S. Katz and Peter Mair (eds.) *How Parties Organize: Change and Adaptation in Party Organizations in Western Democracies.* London: Sage Publications.

McAllister, Ian and Anthony Mughan. 1985. "Attitudes, Issues, and Labour Party Decline in England, 1974-1979." *Comparative Political Studies* 18:37-57.

McKenzie, R.T. 1955. *British Political Parties.* Melbourne: William Heinemann.

Messina, Anthony. 1995. "Are West European Parties in Crisis? Select Evidence from the British and German Cases." Paper presented to the Party Politics Conference, Manchester, U.K., 13-15 January.

Michels, Robert. 1962. *Political Parties: A Sociological Study of the Oligarchical Tendencies of Modern Democracy*. New York: Free Press.

Mileti, Dennis S., David F. Gillespie, and J. Eugene Haas. 1977. "Size and Structure in Complex Organizations." *Social Forces* 56:208-217.

Muller, Wolfgang. 1992. "The Catch-All Party Thesis and the Austrian Social Democrats." *German Politics* 1:181-199.

Muller, Wolfgang C., and Barbara Steininger. 1994. "Party Organisation and Party Competitiveness: The Case of the Austrian People's Party, 1945-1992." *European Journal of Political Research* 26: 1-30.

Muller-Rommel, Ferdinand. 1991. "Small Parties in Comparative Perspective: The State of the Art." In Ferdinand Muller-Rommel and Geoffrey Pridham (eds.) *Small Parties in Western Europe: Comparative and National Perspectives*. London: Sage Publications.

Muller-Rommel, Ferdinand and Geoffrey Pridham (eds.). 1991. *Small Parties in Western Europe: Comparative and National Perspective*. London: Sage Publications.

Olson, Mancur. 1965. *The Logic of Collective Action: Public Goods and the Theory of Groups*. Cambridge: Harvard University Press.

Panebianco, Angelo. 1988. *Political Parties: Organization and Power*. Cambridge: Cambridge University Press.

Patterson, Samuel C., and Gregory Caldeira. 1984. "The Etiology of Partisan Competition." *American Political Science Review* 78:691-707.

Pelletier, Rejean. 1995. "Are Political Parties in Decline?: A Comparison of Political Parties and New Social Movements from a Standpoint of

Materialist and Postmaterialist Values." Paper presented at the Party Politics Conference, Manchester, U.K., 13-15 January.

Pfeffer, Jeffrey and Gerald R. Salancik. 1990. "The Design and Management of Externally Controlled Organizations." In D.S. Pugh (ed.) *Organization Theory: Selected Readings*. London: Penguin.

Pimlott, Ben. 1972. "Does Local Party Organization Matter?" *British Journal of Political Science* 2:381-383.

Pimlott, Ben. 1973. "Local Party Organization, Turnout, and Marginality." *British Journal of Political Science* 3:252-255.

Pizzorno, Alessandro. 1981. "Interest and Parties in Pluralism." In Suzanne D. Berger (ed.) *Organizing Interests in Western Europe*. Cambridge: Cambridge University Press.

Poguntke, Thomas. 1994. "Parties in a Legalistic Culture: The Case of Germany." In Richard S. Katz and Peter Mair (eds.) *How Parties Organize: Change and Adaptation in Party Organizations in Western Democracies*. London: Sage Publications.

Poguntke, Thomas. 1995. "Parties and Society in Western Europe: Declining Linkage?" Paper presented at the Party Politics Conference, Manchester, U.K., 13-15 January.

Powell, G. Bingham. 1982. *Contemporary Democracies*. Cambridge, Massachusetts: Harvard University Press.

Prechel, Harland. 1991. "Irrationality and Contradiction in Organizational Change: Transformation in the Corporate Form of a U.S. Steel Corporation, 1930-1987." *The Sociological Quarterly* 32: 423-445.

Pugh, D.S., D.J. Hickson, C.R. Hinnings, and C. Turner. 1968. "Dimensions of Organization Structure." *Administrative Science Quarterly* 13:65-105.

Raschke, Joachim. 1983. "Political Parties in Western Democracies." *European Journal of Political Research* 11:109-114.

Reiter, Howard L. 1989. "Party Decline in the West: A Skeptic's View." *Journal of Theoretical Politics* 1:325-348.

Russett, Bruce, Hayward R. Alker, Jr., Karl W. Deutsch, and Harold Lasswell. 1964. *World Handbook of Political and Social Indicators*. New Haven: Yale University Press.

Sainsbury, Diane. 1985. "The Electoral Difficulties of the Scandinavian Social Democrats in the 1970s: The Social Bases of the Parties and Structural Explanations of Party Decline." *Comparative Politics* 18:1-19.

Scarrow, Susan. 1991. *Organizing for Victory: Political Party Members and Party Organizing Strategies in Great Britain and West Germany, 1945-1989*. Ph.D. Dissertation, Yale University.

Scarrow, Susan. 1992. "The Organization of Party Membership: How Functions Shape Form." Paper presented at the Workshop on "Democracies and the Organization of Political Parties," ECPR Joint Sessions, University of Limerick, Ireland, 30 March - 4 April.

Scarrow, Susan. 1994. "The 'Paradox of Enrollment': Assessing the Costs and Benefits of Party Memberships." *European Journal of Political Research* 25:41-60.

Scarrow, Susan. 1996. *Parties and their Members: Organizing for Victory in Britain and Germany*. Oxford: Oxford University Press.

Selle, Per and Lars Svasand. 1991. "Membership in Party Organizations and the Problem of Decline of Parties." *Comparative Political Studies* 23: 459-477.

Shaw, Eric. 1988. *Discipline and Discord in the Labour Party*. Manchester: Manchester University Press.

Smith, Gordon. 1991. "In Search of Small Parties: Problems of Definition,

Classification and Significance." In Ferdinand Muller-Rommel and Geoffrey Pridham (eds.) *Small Parties in Western Europe: Comparative and National Perspectives.* London: Sage Publications.

Stimson, James. 1985. "Regression in Space and Time: A Statistical Essay." *American Journal of Political Science* 29:914-947.

Strom, Kaare. 1990. "A Behavioral Theory of Competitive Political Parties." *American Journal of Political Science* 34: 569-98.

Sundberg, Jan. 1992. "Explaining Party Membership Change." Paper presented at the workshop "Democracies and the Organization of Political Parties" ECPR Joint Sessions, University of Limerick, Ireland, 30 March - 4 April.

Taagepera, Rein and Matthew S. Shugart. 1990. *Seats and Votes.* New Haven: Yale University Press.

Tan, Alexander C. 1995. "Party Size, Structure, Participation, and Performance: A Cross-sectional Analysis." Paper presented at the 1995 Annual Meeting of the Western Political Science Association, Portland, Oregon.

Tan, Alexander C. 1997. "Party Change and Party Membership Decline: An Exploratory Analysis." *Party Politics* 3: 363-378.

Tan, Alexander C. 1998. "The Impacts of Party Membership Size: A Cross-national Analysis." *Journal of Politics* 60: 188-198.

Taylor, A.H. 1972. "The Effect of Party Organization: Correlation between Campaign Expenditure and Voting in the 1970 Election." *Political Studies* 20: 329-331.

Tomasko, Robert M. 1987. *Downsizing: Reshaping the Corporation for the Future.* New York: Amacon.

Tsouderos, John E. 1955. "Organizational Change in Terms of A Series of

Selected Variables." *American Sociological Review* 20:206-210.

Von Beyme, Klaus. 1985. *Political Parties in Western Democracies.* New York: St. Martin's Press.

Ware, Alan. 1987. *Citizens, Parties and the State.* Princeton: Princeton University Press.

Ware, Alan. 1996. *Political Parties and Party Systems.* Oxford: Oxford University Press.

Warhurst, John. 1983. "One party or eight parties? The State and Territory Labor Parties." In Andrew Parkin and John Warhurst (eds.) *Machine Politics in the Australian Labor Party.* Sydney: George Allen and Unwin.

Webb, Paul. 1994. "Party Organizational Change in Britain: The Iron Law of Centralization?" In Richard S. Katz and Peter Mair (eds.) *How Parties Organize: Change and Adaptation in Party Organizations in Western Democracies.* London: Sage Publications.

Webb, Paul. 1995. "Are British Political Parties in Decline?" *Party Politics* 1:299-322.

Webber, Douglas C. 1978. "Trade Unions and the Labour Party: The Death of Working-Class Politics in New Zealand." In Stephen Levine (ed.) *Politics in New Zealand: A Reader.* Sydney: George Allen and Unwin.

Weber, Max. 1946. In H.H. Gerth and C. Wright Mills (eds.) *From Max Weber: Essays in Sociology.* New York: Oxford University Press.

Whiteley, Paul F., and Patrick Seyd. 1994. "Local Party Campaigning and Electoral Mobilization in Britain." *Journal of Politics* 56:228-252.

Widfeldt, Anders. 1992. "Development in Party Membership." Paper presented at the Workshop on Democracies and the Organization of Political Parties, ECPR Joint Sessions, University of Limerick, March 30-April 4.

Widfeldt, Anders. 1999. *Linking Parties with People? Party Membership in Sweden 1960-1997*. Aldershot, United Kingdom: Ashgate.

Wolinetz, Steven B. 1990. "The Transformation of Western European Party Systems." In Peter Mair (ed.) *The West European Party System*. Oxford: Oxford University Press.

Wolinetz, Steven B. (ed.). 1998. *Political Parties*. Aldershot, United Kingdom: Dartmouth Publishing.

Appendix I List of Political Parties

Country	Party Name
Australia	Labor Party
	Liberal Party
Austria	People's Party
	Socialist Party
	Freedom Party
Canada	Conservative Party
	Liberal Party
	New Democratic Party
	Social Credit Party
Denmark	Social Democratic Party
	Liberal Party
	Conservative People's Party
	Social Liberal Party (RV)
Germany	Christian Democratic Union
	Free Democratic Party
	Social Democratic Party
Iceland	Independence Party
	Progressive Party
	People's Alliance
	Social Democratic Party
Ireland	Fianna Fail
	Fine Gael
	Labour Party
New Zealand	National Party
	Labour Party
Netherlands	Communist Party
	Labour Party
	Anti-Revolutionary Party
	Christian Historical Union
	Catholic People's Party
	Liberal Party

Sweden   Social Democratic Party
            Center Party
            People's Party
            Moderate Party
U.K.   Conservative Party
            Labour Party

Appendix II Coding Scheme for Leadership Concentration

0   Leadership is so dispersed that only local or regional leaders can be identified; no one presents a serious claim to the position of national party spokesman, much less central decision maker.

1   Leadership is clearly decentralized ; there are more than five leaders who frequently make pronouncements in behalf of the national party but they are not regarded as authoritatively binding spokesmen.

2   Leadership is decentralized; from one to five persons speak in behalf of the party but they are not regarded as authoritatively binding spokesmen by themselves for they do often disagree.

3   Leadership is collectively centralized into a group of more than five party leaders; the decisions of this group are regarded as authoritatively binding on the party; there may be a party leader, but he alone is not powerful enough to control party policy.

4   Leadership is collectively centralized into a group of three to five party leaders: the decisions of this group are regarded as binding on the party.

5   Leadership is shared by two individuals: their joint decisions are regarded as binding on the party.

6   Leadership is exercised by one individual who can personally commit the party to binding courses of action.

Source: Janda 1980